NetworkAbility

NetworkAbility

Building your Business one Relationship at a Time

Helga Henry and Andy Bass

Matador
9 Priory Business Park,
Wistow Road, Kibworth Beauchamp,
Leicestershire. LE8 0RX
Tel:0116 279 2299
Email: books@troubador.co.uk
Web: www.troubador.co.uk/matador
Twitter: @matadorbooks

ISBN 978 1785892 455

British Library Cataloguing in Publication Data.
A catalogue record for this book is available from the British Library.

Printed and bound by CPI Group (UK) Ltd, Croydon, CR0 4YY
Typeset in 11pt Gill Sans Light by Troubador Publishing Ltd, Leicester, UK

Matador is an imprint of Troubador Publishing Ltd

Acknowledgements

Helga Henry
I'd like to thank Mark Ball, Noel Dunne and Lara Ratnaraja who encouraged me to take this material and apply it, to great effect, to the cultural and creative industries; Angela Maxwell, my champion in so many different ways; Dean Melbourne and Gemma Thomas, early enthusiastic adopters of this approach to great effect in their career; Emily Jayne Phillips, Thomasina Carlyle and Grace Morgan from Creative Shift and Sue Smith at Aston University for their support in the publishing of this book. Many thanks to those who have been kind enough to provide endorsements: Andy Street for the Foreword; John Crabtree, OBE, Julia Hobsbawm OBE, Rabbi Julia Neuberger, Siôn Simon MEP and Michael Wolff. And I'd like to acknowledge Hortense Cartwright, a natural builder of relationships and networks from whom I still have much to learn.

Andy Bass
I'd like to thank Paul Clusker, who initially suggested business relationship development as a focus for our work together, and co-presented much of this material to clients in leading professional service firms in the UK, Europe and the CIS; Debbie Jenkins and Joe Gregory, whose work on Lean Marketing provided the basis for our approach to a networking pipeline and the crucial idea of the Most Wanted Response; Alex Bishop and Amardeep Gill, who introduced us to our first clients in their respective firms; and Angela Edkins, who championed the use of this material for students on the Aston MBA programme.

And we would both like to thank Simon and Barbara for their huge support in all that we do.

Contents

Foreword by Andy Street

If you are like me the word "networking" leaves one cold, particularly at huge conferences. However the words, "collaboration", "partnership" or "extended team working" are genuinely exciting in business.

Valuing such relationships is the approach I have tried to take in John Lewis, and latterly in my Chairing of the GBSLEP. Arguably this approach is delivering benefit as, guided by what we call "Team Birmingham", results are flowing for the city region. This book is a practical guide to moving from mere networking to building those more developed structures and relationships.

Helga Henry and Andy Bass may indeed save us all hours in the future!

Andy Street, Managing Director John Lewis and Chair of Greater Birmingham and Solihull LEP

About the Authors

Helga Henry

Helga Henry is Director of Organisational Development at Birmingham Hippodrome, a leading UK theatre, and is also a public speaker, broadcaster and writer. She previously led Creative Shift, a boutique consultancy within the Hippodrome where she worked with a range of corporate clients, cultural organisations, public bodies and Universities. A Clore Fellow in 2008/10, she worked on secondment at St Ann's Warehouse, a flagship theatre venue in Brooklyn, New York. Early in her career she spent 8 years as a solicitor at Wragge & Co (now Gowling WLG).

Helga has served on countless boards of arts charities as a trustee and is currently a Non-Exec Director of the Creative Advantage Fund, the UK's first dedicated VC fund for the creative industries. Her networking expertise has helped large organisations to improve knowledge sharing and collaboration, talented part-time painters to become internationally-recognised artists, and, on one occasion, an events company that had been let down to find, not one, but three alternative sources of Chinese dragons at short notice.

Andy Bass Phd

Andy is the founder and principal of BassClusker Consulting, a leadership and strategy consultancy that helps organisations to do better and faster work with the resources they have already. He has clients across a wide range of industries and sectors including professional services, packaging, technology, health, financial services and education. While based in the UK, Andy travels extensively, and has worked in the US, Europe, Mexico, Russia and China.

Andy has taught at Warwick and Aston Business Schools, and is a visiting faculty member at the Aston Centre for Executive Development. He is a member of the 'Big Thinkers' panel of experts for #oglivychange, the innovative behavioural change practice of Ogilvy & Mather.

Andy has a PhD in software engineering from Aston University. He is author of "The Performance Papers: Incisive Briefings for Busy Leaders", published by Bookshaker, and "Seven Keys To Releasing Potential In Your Business, Your People, And Yourself", available at his website: www.bassclusker.com.

He is a former director of Birmingham Forward and was advisor to the Birmingham Future Mentoring Scheme, through which he helped many ambitious professionals improve their networking results. Outside his work, he enjoys boating, walking and playing the electric guitar.

Website

For tips, downloadable templates, training, coaching or to contact the authors, visit www.networkabilitybook.com

Introduction

What is networking?

Networking is a much misunderstood term. For many, it is entirely synonymous with sales activity and therefore only the concern of those with a sales-based role. For others it is merely frivolous or peripheral: glad-handing or making meaningless smalltalk in a hotel ballroom. Neither view is helpful.

Networking activity is certainly a crucial step in the development of sales, and that is obviously a key benefit. But there are many others. Better networking can mean:

- improved collaboration with colleagues
- more seamless customer experiences
- accelerated adoption of new initiatives
- better, more insightful information about evolving customer and client needs
- you stay on top of industry trends
- recession-proofing of individual careers (the well-connected worker who brings value to the business is rarely the first to be downsized)
- the ability to tap into the hidden job market
- a spring-board into independent consulting and freelancing
- boosted influence and effectiveness for leaders

It can do this because all business is done between people. It's not that Rolls-Royce does business with EADS, but a real person called Mary, with a national insurance number, a family, a dog and a house in Derby does business with Francois, an individual with an INSEE code, three cats and a Gite in Biarritz.

Similarly – and whatever employment law says is supposed to happen – a huge number of job appointments, at all levels from intern to Chairman of the Board, go to people who have or can make a human connection with the person who can say 'Yes' outside of the formal structures set up by HR, recruiters and online recruitment portals.

Inside large organizations – ones big enough for many fellow employees to be strangers - networks are similarly vital. The daily cross-functional friction which costs businesses so much time, energy and reputation – purchases delayed by an officious procurement process, new product launches which seem to struggle to get marketing support, infighting over allocation of budgets, complaining customers passed from pillar-to-post, them-and-us culture clashes post-merger – none of this comes out of nowhere. It all comes down to less-than-collaborative interactions among real people.

In short, networking is about making and maintaining relationships that sustain businesses and careers.

A good network certainly includes people who will buy from you or might hire you. But a really valuable, well-rounded network, rather than simply featuring a database of customers or sales prospects or prospective future employers, also has the following types of people in it:

- Peers with whom you collaborate, share and seek inspiration.
- Mentors or potential mentors who guide your development.

- Mentees who will bring greater satisfaction and a younger perspective to your career.
- Clients and prospective clients (or employers and prospective employers).
- Multipliers – those who are not clients themselves but who can introduce you to number of clients.
- Champions or evangelists – those people who have used your services or products, or who have employed you and who will recommend you.

If you put enough time and energy into growing all elements of your network you will ultimately reach a point where your multipliers and champions will introduce you to other useful and people from the other three categories. This book shows you the steps you need to take to reach this networking "sweet spot".

About this book

We wrote this book because we found that many capable and talented business-people and employees either had the wrong idea about networking or were not using their networking time as effectively as they might. When we introduced them the processes in this book, they immediately felt more focussed about what they were trying to achieve, and more importantly, started to get results.

In business, time is always at a premium. Reading this book should save you valuable time. Much networking takes place out of hours, and 'the day job' will always be there calling you. If you are going to an event in the evening or a breakfast event and effectively extend your working day by a couple of hours, you need to know that the effort will be worthwhile. One thing that will become apparent is that the real networking – the activity that brings you the results you need – starts after you have been to an event or met your new contact.

The first thing to understand is that follow-up is the major part of the game. We will show you what good follow up looks like and give you practical examples of how to do it. It's only once you get systematic in cultivating your network that the hours spent at events and breakfasts will start to pay dividends.

Why 70 days?

We have applied our step-by-step process to this formula to provide a framework for rapid progress and improvement. Your effective network would double in size, your ability to boost sales or increase engagement could be twice as good, if you follow the 70 day plan.

It will be the steady, incremental actions taken consistently that will bring about results. Better to spend ten or fifteen minutes a day on this material every day than a full or half day every six weeks. This starts straight away in Chapter 1 – where we share how to get started, how to use the book and our 70 day success plan.

If you want an instant improvement or speedy results to spur you along, read Chapter 12 – Fifty Ways to Boost Your Networking Immediately.

Who is this book for?

It is hard to think of anyone who couldn't benefit from a better network. The few that come to mind do so because they are already phenomenally well connected.

In general this book is for people who run organizations, people who work for them, and people who want to work for or with them. Specifically, it may be more important for some types of individuals and businesses than others. In our view, you should be sure to prioritise putting time and energy into networking if:

- You are a fee-earning professional in a large firm providing professional or business support services (law, accountancy, property consulting, engineering consulting etc)
- You run, or want to run a small, expertise-based or creative firm, consultancy or personal service practice.
- You want to increase your success in a corporate career.
- You want to increase your organisation's ability to learn, respond and innovate in a fast-paced business environment.

Clearly network building skills have wide application and are useful for most people. It's helpful to narrow things down. To learn more about the particular benefits of networking depending on your situation (and there is no particular need to read the sections that don't immediately apply to you) please refer to the sections in Appendix I.

If you are a senior executive

Why does this matter to senior executives? Some of the top reasons are:

- To avoid getting get caught in a bubble
- To get ideas from non-competing peers in different industries
- To learn from and influence stakeholders in investor groups, government, regulatory authorities and the media.
- To understand what it takes to foster networking among their people, in order to win contracts, foster collaboration and engagement.

Chapter 11 is specifically about the benefits that can accrue from pursuing networking as a source of competitive advantage, and you might want to read it first, and then go back to look at earlier chapters, particularly Chapters 8 and 9 to get a sense of the overall programme.

I'm convinced! Where do I start?

Chapter 1 gives you an overview of the book, the steps you need to take and a suggested 70 day action plan. It provides a framework for the subsequent chapters and lets you see how those steps fit into an overall structure provided in Chapter 2.

However you decide to use this book we hope that you enjoy the process of building your business relationships, giving value to get value and possibly open your life up to new experiences and opportunities. Using this process has helped up build our businesses, find new partners and collaborators and even build a friendship or two.

Most of all, we hope that the tools in this book will give you access to the men and women who will help your business or career thrive based on your talents and hard work rather than your starting 'position' in society.

You can access useful articles, checklists and further information including dates where Helga and Andy are speaking on this topic at www.NetworkAbilitybook.com. It is updated with relevant content to enhance your understanding and inspire you to fulfil all 70 days of this practical programme.

Chapter 1

NetworkAbility – Getting Started

Do you really need to network? Whatever your role, the short answer is probably 'Yes', and we realise that you may or may not be delighted by that! But we also know from long experience that for most people, any reluctance they feel is actually more about not knowing how to do it than any deep objection on principle.

Fortunately, networking can be made straightforward – this book will show you exactly how. Before we get to the skills though, it is worth spending some time on getting the right mindset to make it easy.

The False Choice Reluctant Networkers Must Reject

Here are some typical remarks about the importance, or otherwise, of relationships in business:

> *"I have no time for that marketing bullshit. In my day you got work by being good! Mind you, Sir Alan does say that I couldn't sell a box of matches to a smoker." (Margaret from The Apprentice, former Partner at leading law firm Herbert Smith, in an interview in The Lawyer magazine)*

> *"There are two types of people in any organisation, those who get on by adding value, and those who get on based on who they have curried favour with." (frustrated senior manager at a global financial institution)*

> *"It's not what you know, it's who you know." (anon.)*

All of these assume an either-or choice: succeed based on merit, or based on your contacts. But what if the choice is a false one? Here are five reasons why we think it is:

1. In every field, there are talented people who never get anywhere because noone has heard of them. We have both met many such frustrated and puzzled people, and have often coached them to start having the impact they deserve.

2. If noone knows it, then does it matter how good you are? Maybe if you are a monk, but are you up for taking the vow of poverty? A few years ago, the musician and producer Ry Cooder made a film called Buena Vista Social Club about a group of Cuban musicians who had been performing in their home country for decades but who were unknown in the outside world. The film was a huge hit and it opened up all kinds of possibilities for the musicians concerned to perform internationally, work with top musicians around the world, and certainly to improve their standard of living substantially. Without their connection to Ry Cooder, they would have carried on being great in obscurity.

3. If you genuinely are better than those who are getting on because of their schmoozing, then don't you owe it to yourself (and everyone else) to get your contribution out there? Most of us have worked in organizations where bad managers have been promoted to positions where they have a damaging effect, just because they knew the right people. If you want good managers in your organization, you need to develop the skills yourself and make sure you get the chance to use them.

4. How do you come up with anything new if you don't interact in the marketplace and with colleagues from different disciplines?

If you cut yourself off from the outside world, or just get your news pre-packaged by industry journalists, you will end up in a hall of mirrors. The way to improve is to constantly test ideas by chatting with customers, clients, suppliers, colleagues and as varied a set of opinion-formers as you can find.

5. To be creative or innovative, you need the best possible dialogue and feedback. Charles Darwin used to have a transatlantic correspondence with Ben Franklin. If these two 'giants' thought they benefited from networking, can you dismiss the idea as simply schmoozing?

Before We Get Started: What About The Old Boy's Network?

It is often said that "It's not what you know, but who you know". The "old boy network" which gave rise to that cliché is on the wane – a very good thing. Before equal opportunities legislation, certain professions and organizations were effectively closed shops with entry and favour based not on absolute talent and ability, but on family connections, or where you lived or were educated.

Such factors still exert a strong influence, albeit more discreetly, and they always will. But today it is much easier for those born without privilege to build the considerable advantage of a well-rounded network of people who will help their talents, their business or their career flourish.

Getting Started: How To Use This Book

We hope that we have convinced you to take the next steps to books your networking and accrue the many benefits that a well-rounded business network can bring.

The chapters of this book can be used as a self-guided study programme to build your networking and business relationships at your own pace. If you want to make more rapid progress we propose a 70 day action plan at the end of this chapter.

Time spent on reconnaissance is seldom wasted

This military adage extols the virtues of taking stock of your surroundings and ascertaining your starting position before launching an attack. A few moments to familiarise yourself with the premises of this book and its overall approach may be helpful at this point.

The first thing to do, regardless of your level of networking experience is to read Chapter 2 and gain an overview of the way that business relationships develop over time. This forms the spine of our approach. Sharing this backbone of our thinking with clients over time has generated a number of insights – suddenly they see the whole picture rather than focussing on their shyness, a reluctance to be in a crowd of strangers or the business card swap (which we also cover later). The rapidity of the progress – from stranger to client (or employer), from Free to Fee – is not necessarily a result of the effluxion of time but the fulfilment of certain criteria or conditions. Knowing the stage of progress that you have reached with a given contact will help you plan your tactics to move them on in a targeted, more effective way.

You have the route – where to begin?

Chapter 2 gives the route to your ultimate destination – the result that you seek from making a connection. The next step is to locate where you are right now: Chapter 3 will allow you to assess your current NetworkAbility level by self-diagnosis from the descriptions of the five levels of networker we have identified in the past. To give you a more specific metric you can complete the Personal Skills checklist in Chapter 3.

The next stage is to map your network as this can guide your subsequent actions – Chapter 4 encourages you to collate your network into one place. A database of people with their contact details and other information will allow you to put them into the categories that constitute a well rounded network. Once all your disparate addresses, business cards, beermats and emails are in one place you can assess which of the network categories are underpopulated or relatively weak. You will gain a sense of who (or the types of people) to target in building your network.

Then you can (and here's a key secret) choose a networking location that will optimise the chances of your meeting the types of people you want to meet. Chapter 4 provides some ideas of where to meet people. In short – if you hang out where the people you want to meet hang out and engage in respectful, value building conversations with them, you will immediately improve your chances of improving your network (by which we mean by meeting and doing business with the right contacts for you).

Conversation and listening skills

Depending on your NetworkAbility score and your overall goals you may need to:

- Build your confidence
- Work on your "small talk" in order to initiate a mutually profitable dialogue/conversation
- Work on your listening skills (check out the section in Chapter 6 on ELIZA technique and "hot words")

- Find a mentor (see Chapter 9)
- Know how to move the conversation from social topics to business topics (Chapter 7)
- Navigate common networking niggles – joining a seemingly closed group, entering a room full of strangers or extricating yourself from a conversation (all covered in Chapter 7).

Whatever your NetworkAbility score, everyone needs to:

- Understand what they are trying to achieve over a reasonable timescale
- Choose appropriate locations in line with their priorities (Chapter 4)
- Select who to prioritise (Chapter 8, Assessing Contact Quality)
- Understand and adopt the pipeline approach (Chapter 9)
- Move those contacts through the pipeline
- Having met someone, follow up fast, frequently and intelligently (Chapters 8 and 9)
- Review and update periodically their pipeline or network map in order to set new targets.

Finally, for business owners, leaders and managers there are chapters on how to instil a networking culture in your organisation, division or tem (Chapter 10) and some thoughts on improving employee performance through networking (Chapter 11).

If You Don't Have 70 Days

Head straight for Chapter 12, it has fifty hints and tips that can instantly boost your networking performance.

If You Do Have 70 Days

The grid below is a suggested daily action plan – based on Alan Weiss's observation that suggested incremental 1% improvements will double your ability in 70 days. Twice as good in 70 days? We will let you decide!

Week	Monday	Tuesday	Wednesday	Thursday	Friday
1	Read Chapter 2	Read Chapter 3 Order business cards if needed	Complete Personal Skills Checklist page 44	Pull all your contacts into one searchable place and create back up	Assess your network map and create list of targets – see page 51
2	Read Chapter 4 Get some good head shots to use in your online profiles	Start to research networking opportunities and locations	Identify potential mentor for networking project and contact them	Chose locations where you are likely to meet your targets	Read Chapters 5 and 6 – you are ready to go out networking!
3	Create an online presence that aggregates information about you – blog/website or LinkedIn profile	Read Chapters 8 and 9 to understand follow up Assess contact quality – see page 117	Create first draft of pipeline document page 25	Research the social networks that are used by your peers and targets – spend a little time just "lurking"	Research any conferences or trade shows, missions or trips that may be appropriate. Identify who to meet there.
4	Meet your mentor some time this week to set up the relationship	Practice questioning with a direction in mind (ideally at a networking event otherwise just socially)	Practice "hot words" exercise on page 89 (you are networking by now aren't you? If not – start!)	Subscribe to business magazine or newsfeed as relevant	Practice small talk with people you don't know in a safe setting
5	Follow up e-mails – info and suggest coffee/ second meeting if you haven't already	Write an article, briefing, newsletter or blog post of interest to your targets	Update your database if you haven't done so as you go along	Scroll through the contacts on your phone and call someone you haven't contacted for a while just to say hello	Check your diary –any events upcoming to which you can invite a contact?

6	Set up a couple of lunches with former colleagues or peers you haven't seen	Collate or list useful links and articles etc that you have written	Consider networking targets in your own organisation and arrange a coffee	Attend an appropriate event that you have never been to before to meet new people	Review your progress: ask three questions (see page 121). Celebrate your successes
7	Assess how well you can move from "Social General" to "Business General" conversation	Note down any great questions you have asked or been asked recently	Get your news from a new or different source today: different journal, TV channel or feed	Be a broker: arrange a lunch for two mutual contacts who you know need to meet. Pick up the tab.	Offer to speak or contribute to an event relevant to your sector or your goals.
8	Arrange to catch up with old friend or someone who has fallen off your radar	Re-read Chapters 5 and 6 to refresh your memory on conversation techniques	Create/collate some valuable collateral for sharing – top tips, checklists and guidance	Research some of the general business topics of interest using PESTLE (see page 101)	Focus on positive outcomes – list five key successes so far for you
9	Write an article, briefing, newsletter or blog post of interest to your targets.	Think about your champions or multipliers – have you thanked them recently?	Introduce or recommend a peer of yours to a contact who needs their input or services	Set a challenge to listen twice as much as you speak (or vice versa as needed) at your next event	Update your pipeline document if you haven't already
10	Consider becoming a mentor to someone else to support them	Visit a new group as a guest or attend a different type of event – gallery opening or sports	Meet with your mentor for a progress report	Check your diary –any events upcoming to which you can invite a contact?	Review your progress: ask three questions (see page 121). Celebrate your successes
11	Read Chapter 12 and try out 3 ideas in the next week.	Are you still leaving people in a better state than you found them? If not review page 77	Identify potential volunteering or committee work and approach organisers	Ask one of your new contacts to recommend a good, useful place to network and go there	Propose a relevant article for a local paper, trade journal or internal magazine

12	Assess your network for its diversity: do you need move some contacts to "holding"?	If attending a conference – contact speakers in advance to see if you can meet	Nominate someone you admire in your network for a relevant business award	How are your listening skills developing? Review ELIZA and Hot Words (p 87 onwards)	Review your pipeline document and update – are your targets "moving on"?
13	Review where you get your information – add add or change your subscriptions and feeds	Search for your name online to manage your online reputation if necessary	Scroll through the contacts on your phone and call someone you haven't contacted for a while just to say hello	Do you need more business cards?	Write an article, briefing, newsletter or blog post of interest to your targets.
14	Re-do your Personal Skills Checklist – are your progressing? What do you want to work on next?	Consider networking with some new targets in your own organisation and arrange a coffee	Write to us to share your success story and how we can improve this book	Take your mentor to a "Thank You" lunch	Review your progress. Celebrate your wins and keep going!

Final Thoughts

A friend of ours loves an old French saying to the effect: "If the young knew, if the old could." Networking can be a slow burner which means that if you are still waiting to get started: stop waiting! Put the ideas in this book into practice and start to get the benefits as soon as possible.

Chapter 2

How Business Relationships Develop – The Big Picture

In Chapter 1 we talk about how to get started. In this chapter we want to give you the big picture about how business relationships are built and nurtured. Once you understand this chapter, you will have the framework in which to slot the specific advice, tools and techniques we cover later. There is also some guidance as to what to do in situations that we have not explicitly covered. Our clients typically report that once they know the material in this chapter, they get a completely new view of networking. It becomes a much more approachable and manageable endeavour.

So, here we are going to answer two of the most fundamental questions to ask once you start to get serious about networking:

- What needs to happen for me to build a relationship with a new person?
- For contacts I already have, what do I do to develop the relationship further?

Many people are much perplexed by these questions. One law firm partner made the following observation:

> *"When I started out as a young lawyer in the City of London, it was quite different to the way it is now. Frankly we could sit behind our desks and the work would just roll in. I never needed to network, and because I have a reputation now, I still don't need to that much. But it's so different now."*
>
> *"I'll tell you the real problem. It's not so much that it's uncomfortable for those of us who are more introverted. I*

mean, it is sometimes, but usually I find that when I make the effort and go to an event, people are perfectly pleasant. I usually leave thinking 'that wasn't so bad after all.'"

"OK, fine. But it's the second thought that troubles me: 'Ok, I've been networking. I put in an appearance. I can tick a checkbox for the marketing department. But: I have no idea whether I have just used my time well, or wasted it totally. People were nicer than I expected, but so what? Would I have been better to spend that hour-and-a-half working on something billable? Or would I have been better going home and spending the time with my family who are constantly complaining about how little time they see me? I simply don't know."

There was no link in his mind between what he was calling his networking and any kind of return on investment. He suspected it was something he should be doing, but didn't know how to make it more than just an ineffectual box-ticking exercise.

The following sections demonstrate a way to fix that disconnect.

Working Backwards To Create Steps Forwards

The bottom line is that someone you just met in a hotel ballroom or company away-day is not likely to give you a huge contract, a solid referral or a major shift in internal resources to support your initiative – it's simply far too big a step. Joe Gregory and Debbie Jenkins (authors of the lean marketing handbook *The Gorillas Want Bananas*) have a simple and clear way of picturing this:

The new contact is on the ground. Rather than expecting that they will expend the huge effort required to climb onto the wall in one go, it's better to ask them to take a step at a time:

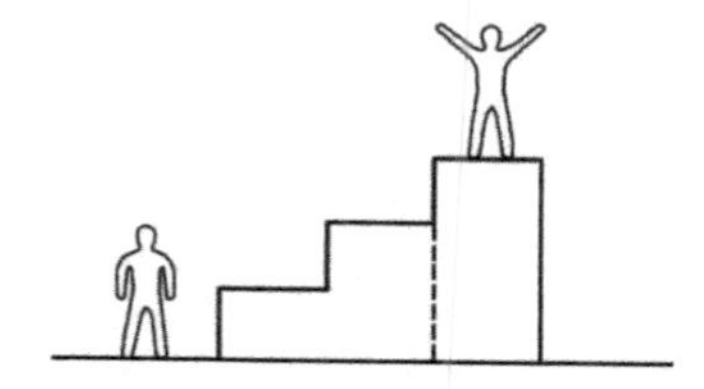

If you break those steps down systematically, you will see how much more manageable the process can be, and you will have a much better idea about your objectives if you do go to an event in the proverbial ballroom.

Let's start with the most tangible and measurable reason for networking outside your organisation – quite simply to meet new people to sell a product or service to in order to get paid some money. For those networking inside their organisation the motivation may be to find collaborators on a project, support for an initiative or resources to help you attain your corporate objectives. Here's the situation many inexperienced networkers find themselves in.

In this diagram the bag with the "£" represents the result you are seeking to achieve: a sale (a "buy"), a collaboration, a "yes" to an integration project or proposal (a "buy-in")

Obviously it's far too big a distance to cover in one jump. People who try and make that jump just end up putting people off.

The trick is to break this down and work backwards. So let's start at the desired end of the process. We agree that our objective is a payment or result. And in order to get that result, someone is going to have to accept a proposal from us (or you can call it a 'quote', or 'offer' – the name doesn't matter) so that we can deliver something to them or work with them.

In most businesses you won't be making proposals to people you have just met. But here is the magic question: who could you easily and naturally make a proposal to? What kind of situation would make that possible? In terms of the picture, what's the stepping stone just before someone agrees to buy or to buy-in?

Well, imagine if someone has an urgent requirement that they need fulfilling. It might be for legal advice, or for a new website, or for anything really. If they are of the opinion that you are the right person, and the need is urgent, wouldn't it be easy to make a proposal that you do the work? You wouldn't need any 'sales techniques'. You could just say something like, "Why don't I put a proposal together and send it over, and then call you on Friday to see what you think?"

Well that's fine as far as it goes, except it's still a long way from where we start in that ballroom or away day. So we need to apply the same kind of thinking again. What is the kind of situation in which someone would be prepared to discuss a concrete bit of work with you, to give you some kind of formal meeting where you could learn sufficient detail to establish that you are indeed the person for the job? (By the way, when we say 'formal' meeting, it doesn't mean you have to be suited-and-booted in the boardroom. We know someone who got a major assignment while talking to a client on a chairlift in Aspen. What made it formal was that there was a serious prospect of work on the table at the time).

In pictorial form, here is what we are now asking:

Under what conditions would you easily be able to suggest a formal meeting? You can put it in your own words, but we would say that it was simply that they think you are likely to be able to help with whatever is of concern to them.

Like this:

Again, let's recognise that it is likely to be tough to do it in five minutes at a first meeting at a networking or internal event! So again we need to take another step in our backward reasoning and ask ourselves what is going to have to happen for us demonstrate that we are likely to be able to help?

Typically, it's going to involve one or more informal contacts (which could be face-to-face conversations or exchanges of notes or emails, or phone calls, or many other ways). We will deal with the detail of how to do this in Chapter 8.

Now how are we going to get those informal contacts to happen?

Why would a busy person be prepared to give you informal time for coffees etc? Well, ask yourself why you do it for someone else: isn't it because you are, for some reason, interested to learn more?

If you think a person might have value for you, you will naturally be prepare to learn more about them and what they have to offer, especially if it's low-key and involves a small amount of time and low commitment:

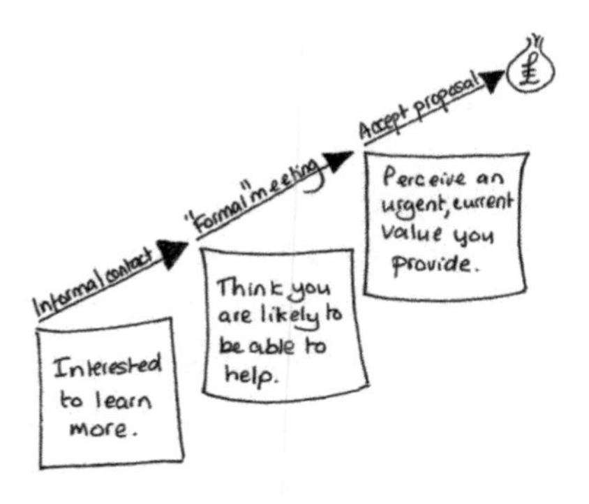

Clearly if someone is interested to hear more about our work, they will be willing to read things we send them, to take a phone call or to meet for a cup of coffee. Building that interest will be the subject of Chapters 7 and 8.

Permission To Contact

Now you can see that we only have room for one more step. At last we are in the original situation. Let's work backwards one more time. How do we create the interest to learn more? Somehow we are going to have to offer some appealing and easy-to-assimilate information, and to do that, we have at a minimum to get to the point where they are happy for us to contact them. Especially with senior, busy and popular people, that is not a trivial matter. If we get their permission to contact them again, we have made definite progress in our ambition to build a relationship.

So now we have the answer to the lawyer's question: "How do I know if I wasted my time or not at that event?"

> *If you got permission to re-contact even one genuine potential client or other valuable member of your network, then you have done well at an event. Getting such permission should be your main (perhaps only) aim at events.*

(By the way, the symbol of permission is the business card. Inexperienced people give out cards willy-nilly, but if you get the card of someone senior, you have done well. Handing out a stack of your own cards doesn't amount to much of an achievement.) So if you are looking for new business, your objective at an event is to get a card from someone who can, one day, give you that business or otherwise refer you to someone who can. So why would someone busy grant you this permission?

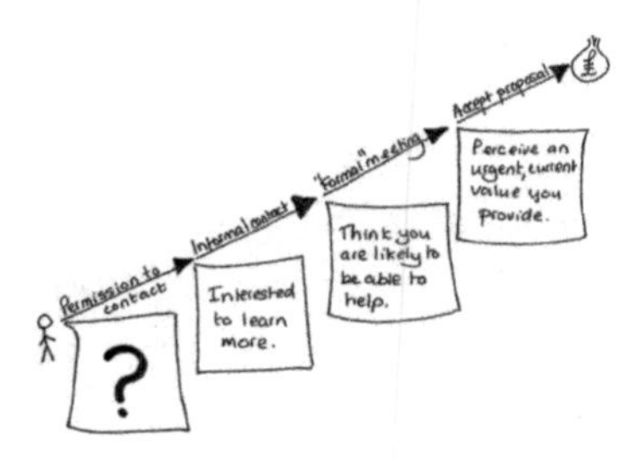

They will need to have formed a particular kind of positive impression and be left thinking that your brand of help could be relevant and useful. How to do that in detail is the subject of Chapters 6 and 7.

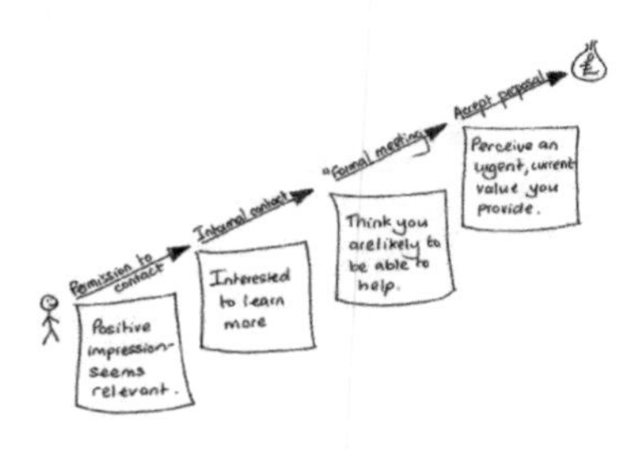

OK, now we have got a clear set of steps.

The great thing about this approach is it shows you exactly what you need to do to make progress, but it avoids you needing to be pushy.

Instead of worrying about pushing people to give you meetings or accepting proposals, you put your effort into creating the conditions in which doing so is the most natural thing in the world.

You shift from selling to learning about them, and educating them about you. To sum it up, at each step, you create the conditions for the next step by providing value.

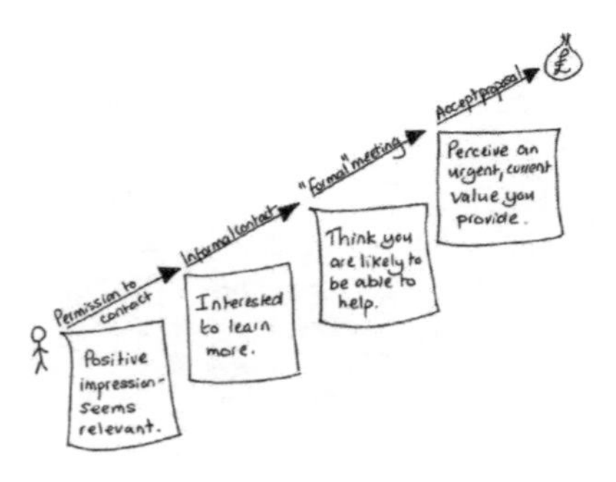

The better you get at this, the less you need to push. In fact in most cases you will get **progress along the path simply by asking.**

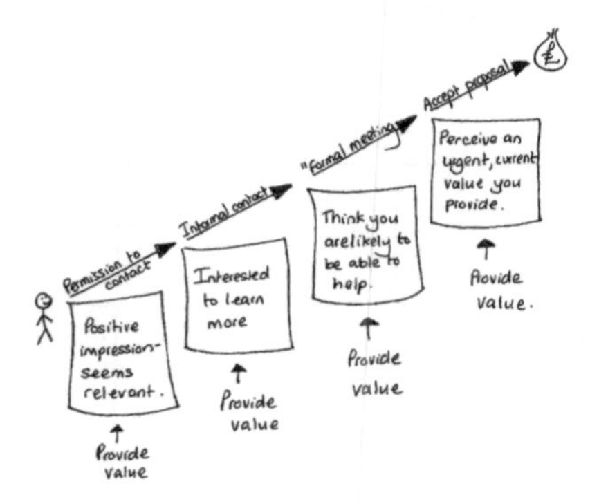

You will feel more comfortable, and so will they.

A Tidied Up Version: The Contact-to-Client Pipeline (external)

Below is a tidied-up version of the build-up we have just done. It's called the Contact-to-Client pipeline, and you will see that the first four columns correspond to what we have just discussed.

The Contact-to-Client Pipeline

Stranger	Knows Who You Are	Actively Networks With You	Is a Potential Client	Has Paid For Work	Repeat Client	Network Multiplier	Champion
Wanted: Permisson to contact them. Their business card.	Wanted: Will give you time for a quick meeting. Will take a call	Wanted: Will seriously consider a specfic proposal	Wanted:	Wanted:	Wanted:	Wanted:	Wanted:
Requires: Has a positive impression	Requires: Is open to finding out more about your work	Requires: They recognise your potential value to them and/or thier contacts	Requires: They recognise a specific, currently relevant value you offer.	Requires:	Requires:	Requires:	Requires:
Tatics:	Tactics:	Tactics	Tactics:	Tactics	Tactics	Tactics:	Tactics

FREE → FEE

Final Thoughts

Each step from meeting a new contact to nurturing a long-term profitable business relationship involves a series of exchanges. To start with these will most likely be small: you give them something (e.g. information, an article, some free advice) and they give you something in return (e.g. their time for a conversation, a meeting, advice). You get a chance to find out what would be of greater value to each other, to do a trade, and demonstrate your ability to deliver something. Along the way, you build up trust and shared understandings.

It should now be clear that:

- A business card is a token of permission to contact someone again
- There is networking before the card swap (that bit that most people think of as the whole game).
- The real networking happens *after* the card-swap.
- Your only aim when attending an event for new business should simply be to get permission to contact high-quality contacts.
- Once you have some such contacts, you turn your attention to moving them through the pipeline systematically.

Many of the following chapters will offer you approaches to moving people through your pipeline. With the comforting thought that the threshold of competence on first meeting someone is relatively low – after all you simply need to leave a positive impression and seem relevant (seem relevant! You don't even have to BE relevant!) – you can explore the skills and attitudes that will boost your NetworkAbility.

Chapter 3

What's your NetworkAbility?

Your NetworkAbility can be considered to be a measure of your efficacy and efficiency in building relationships in order to fulfil your objectives. As previously discussed those objectives might be building sales, boosting collaboration or increasing engagement or any combination of the three. Personal motivations might include career progression or contributing to a social goal for a cause you support.

Whatever your reasons, the way to increase your NetworkAbility is first to assess your skills in the area, your level of competence and confidence. We provide some tools for you to make this assessment in this chapter. Then you can map your network and identify the gaps. Once you identify the gaps you can create targets and chose your locations – this is covered in Chapter 4 and beyond.

Here are the questions you will be able to answer:

- To the extent that I network already, what level am I operating at?
- What skills do I need to develop to improve my ability?

Learning to network well (i.e. so that business or results flow reliably from it) is a skill that takes most people considerable sustained effort. It's also an important process in the development of a well-rounded employee or entrepreneur who can make a long-term contribution to the financial success of a business – and therefore has strategic importance. Over the time we have been working with a variety of businesses and individuals to increase the work that flows from their networking activities, we have come to think in terms of a ladder of levels of effectiveness of networking.

Figure 3.1 Networking levels for internal and external networking

	Internal	External
Level 5	Creates robust team-to-team networks for ongoing collaboration or repeat business	
Level 4	Has a network which yields consistent results	
Level 3	Networks but cannot consistently produce desired results	Networks as a true peer of their contacts
Level 2	Knows people socially	Basically organised networker
Level 1	Stays at desk or within team Few relationships outside direct report	a) Tongue-tied, reluctant networker b) Social butterfly

We've observed frequent attempts to improve performance by trying to apply "the right tool at the wrong level" – typically with limited results. In particular, there is a tendency to rely too much on training events. Training is often extremely useful in improving networking results, but it's rarely sufficient on its own. If you are serious about achieving transformational performance in this area you would consider a programme of events including:

- Skills training for the majority of staff at all levels including a follow up session to pick up questions, queries and show how to develop the pipeline

- Mentoring for key individuals from a diverse range of business areas who can champion the approach throughout the organisation

- Sessions to populate pipelines with live case studies and to create solutions for pipeline "blockages"

- Coaching for managers/senior executives to support the networking function of their direct reports

- Specially tailored events at which relationships can be formed and developed over time.

In order to apply the right approaches, it's important to identify the current stage at which participant individuals and teams find themselves.

In the following sections we discuss each of the five levels, make suggestions about the challenges they pose, and highlight some of the methods that are effective in meeting those challenges. There is nothing sacrosanct about five levels, and others may prefer to carve networking levels up differently, but we find this ladder often helps people to identify where they are, and provides a springboard for a useful discussion.

Level 1a: Tongue-Tied, Reluctant Networker

If you are here, then the thought of going into a business social function probably scares the life out of you! We find that people at this level will do anything to avoid networking, including denying their fear and coming up with plausible-sounding rationales for avoiding it ("too much client work", "I'm a professional, not a salesperson" etc). They typically have an overly simplistic view of networking and if they have any idea of what they are being asked to do at all, they think it's something to do with 'working a room' and giving out business cards, and thereby mysteriously getting work.

Because the idea is inaccurate, the decision that it is impossible is pretty much correct, and any false-starts tend to reconfirm the belief. The first thing you need if you are in this situation is an understanding of an effective process of business development so that it seems do-able, acceptable and manageable.

Level 1B: Social Butterfly

Contrary to what the tongue-tied think, many extroverts are actually not effective networkers. The reason? Well they're so busy having lovely conversations about holidays, football etc that the other person fails to think of them as a business contact. They often end up making pure social acquaintances, or if the other person is senior, they are politely dismissed as lightweight (almost always without realising it has happened). This is often a particular problem for PR and design firms because they hire lots of young, outgoing people who may have to modify their conversational style (or the topics they cover) in order to develop more substance.

Sometimes we have found that the initially tongue-tied overtake the social butterflies once they get some skills, because they are actually more focused on why they are there (and as far as they are concerned, it's not for fun!).

If you are a very sociable person, you may have to deal with these challenges:

- Overcoming your natural tendency to chat without a direction
- Learning to focus on finding out if there is a basis for doing business or helping each other (e.g. through referrals, information), without being pushy.
- Remembering to follow through and pursue the pipeline in an organised diligent fashion rather than moving on to the "next new thing".

Level 2: Basically Organised Networker

You are at Level 2 if:

- You are confident enough to attend events and functions, get into conversations and swap cards
- You understand how events fit into the overall process of business development (and so have a clear idea of why you are there and what you are trying to achieve)
- You correctly put more emphasis on cultivating relationships beyond the initial meeting than just meeting lots of new people
- You know where you are with a particular developing contact, and know what the next step will be in the process.

Such basically organised networkers are surprisingly rare in our experience – many who think they are at this level are actually just experienced social butterflies.

The big challenge for people genuinely at Level 2 has to do with time, your own and that of the people you want to follow up with. In particular, you may struggle:

- to figure out how to give value in order to get value
- to get people to commit time to follow-up meetings

- with your own personal organisation, prioritisation and discipline.

If you are here, then in order to move to the next stage, you need to learn to be seen as a source of value so that your contacts will take your calls, respond to your emails and take time to meet with you.

Level 3: Establishes Genuine Peer-To-Peer Business Relationships

The transition to Level 3 is a true watershed, and once people make it, their networking becomes dramatically more effective.

Here is the issue: people who are senior enough to actually authorise a buying decision are typically under huge time pressure (as are the people who control internal resources), and are having to fend off demands for attention from their own clients, their staff, their other professional advisors, your competitors, people selling them other things etc. Even if they are social extroverts themselves, they simply don't have time for chit-chat. How do you get them to spend some time to allow you to develop a relationship?

Essentially, they have to feel that it's of value for them to do so. The challenge for you if you are at this level is to be thought of as a business peer of the prospective buyer. While not necessarily an expert on all areas of the other person's business (which is hard if you are meeting people from a range of occupations), as a solid Level 3 networker, you will be able to converse on a range of business issues (not just your own area), and will usually be able to find a commercial topic of interest to the other party. You can also relate your follow-up suggestions and invitations to the business needs that really matter to your contact.

In order to make the transition to Level 3, people's requirements can vary hugely. According to their skills, experience and current acumen, you may benefit from a mixture of enhanced business education, directed reading, news summarising services, training in conversational 'tricks-of-the-trade' and ongoing group and/or individual coaching.

Level 4: Actually Gets to Yes

Getting business cards, meticulously following up, having informal conversations, even being thought of as a peer are all nice. But we've worked with people who are stuck at Level 3 because they are great at building solid relationships, but can't translate them into business.

There are a number of reasons which could see you finding it difficult to transition to Level 4, which can include:

- Reluctance to ask for business
- Building relationships with the wrong people
- Dealing with the right person but demonstrating insufficient value to be compelling.

Reluctance to ask for the business should be avoided if you follow the approach we are recommending, but if you find it persists, then we think it is best dealt with on a one-to-one basis, as the block will tend to have an emotional component which can more comfortably be discussed in a confidential setting. The other problems affect all people involved in selling to a greater or lesser degree, and a group can be great for debriefing meetings and brainstorming new ideas to reach the person.

The vastly influential management thinker Peter Drucker always recommended investing in strengths. This is the key to developing excellence (in contrast to the more usual strategy of giving attention and resources to problems – which just raises the average level of performance a bit). People who can close business are perhaps the greatest asset a professional firm can have – therefore it's a skill you should be cultivating. Just as Wimbledon champions still have coaches, there's a lot to be said for continuing your development as a high performer.

Level 5: Creates A Team Approach For Long-Term Ongoing Collaboration

So far we have been talking about your own individual networking. Our guess is that you will probably be able to place yourself quite easily in one of these four levels. But there is one more level to mention that will apply if you are one of those people who are involved not only in winning work but then in handing it on to a team (typically more senior people in all sorts of businesses offering professional and expert services, for example).

Many service industry businesses have the problem that a few partners or owner/managers do all the business development. In larger corporations and institutions the equivalent "rainmaking" activity is left to senior executives or corporate level. They bring the work (or project or funding as appropriate) back to a large bunch of fledglings (and, if we are honest, their less effective colleagues) with hungry open beaks.

Level 5 networking is about shifting attention from the individual 'little black book' of a few star 'rainmakers' to the relationships of the business as a whole. It is particularly powerful in dealing with large clients who have the potential to provide multiple concurrent projects and typically have multiple decision makers and influencers. For example we've done work to help clients in systematically strengthening relationships among professionals of all levels at the firm with key influencers and decision-makers at large financial institutions. We will go into the details of the well-networked organisation in Chapter 11, but here's a taster so you can be thinking about it while you read on. A typical process might involve:

- A programme to get juniors up to level 2/3 as quickly as possible
- Mapping the current relationships on some form of display
- Rating the current stage of development of those relationships
- Displaying the combined relationship in such a way to show current strengths, gaps and opportunities
- Identifying stakeholders' motivations and influence-relationships throughout the whole network.
- Developing actions with the best chance of strengthening those relationships
- Coaching individuals to execute plans as required
- Updating the display as a group to plan the next initiatives.

In addition to increased sales over a relatively short time period, other benefits accrue which enhance the longer term outlook:

- Senior or executive time is freed up to concentrate on the highest value buyers
- Those charged with business development meet people through juniors, as well as the reverse
- Clients perceive that they are dealing with a very strong team
- Juniors are involved in real business development from an early stage.

As we have said we will have more suggestions for managers later. For now, let's return to the individual networker, and help you to identify more clearly exactly what to work on in order to get to your next level.

Confidence

Invariably someone at our sessions will tell us that they are convinced of the need to build relationships and that they will go out and network "when they get some confidence".

The curious thing is that the phrase "get some confidence" makes confidence a commodity – an artifact that ***anyone*** could have, if only they knew which shop or website that stocked it.

Whenever asked, "Where can you get that confidence? Order it online from buymesomeconfidence.com?" People shake their heads: "No, it comes from within…" they acknowledge.

But confidence is not something you ***are***, it's something you do. Olympic cycling coach Steve Peters in his motivational book *The Chimp Paradox* states that we can base our confidence in one of two ways:

"I am basing my confidence on my ability to reach certain levels that I have to achieve and I cannot deal with the consequences of not reaching them."

OR

"I am basing my confidence on doing my best to reach certain levels that I would like to achieve and as an adult **I can always deal with any consequences of not reaching them**."

The key thing about the second approach is that confidence is entirely within your control: confidence comes from the willingness to try something, safe in the knowledge that, you have the mental and emotional resources to deal with the consequences.

This means that you can build your confidence, not just by preparation, learning skills and gaining experience but by amending your approach and making confidence something that is engendered and measured from within. It sits on a foundation of competence which is something you can work on.

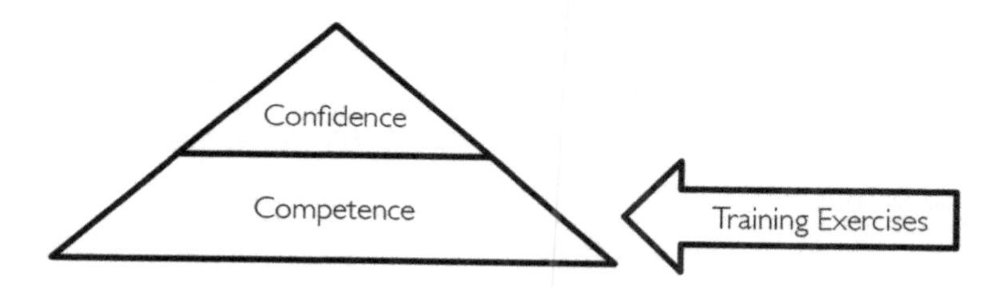

"Just Be Yourself" – Is That Really The Answer?

Often people who find small talk hard receive the advice: "Just be yourself". Is this advice sound?

Well, yes and no. Obviously pretending to be something or someone you are not is fraught with problems, and is hardly likely to lead to sound relationships as time goes by. On the other hand, as a piece of advice "Just be yourself" has a major difficulty:

It doesn't actually tell you what to DO or SAY when you walk into a social gathering, networking meeting or reception. So how do we resolve the confusion?

This popular piece of advice isn't WRONG, but it is operating on the wrong level to be helpful. It's common to confuse who we ARE (our identity) with what we DO (our behaviour). We often hear people who find small talk difficult tell us, "It's just the kind of person I am", almost as if it's genetic.

Yet if we put someone at the wheel of a car without having had any driving lessons, we would not accept the idea that they couldn't drive "because they're not that kind of person". Driving is a skill, not an identity. And we expect to have to learn skills. And this is true of communication as well. Children have to learn not only to speak, but also how to USE language: to make requests, to ask interesting questions, to 'be polite', and so on.

To learn a skill well, we need the *right kind of instruction* and the *right kind of practice*. And communication is a skill most of us learn in a haphazard way, according to our varied experiences growing up. Children do an amazing job of language learning. If their parents speak a different language in the home than the national language, the children learn BOTH and somehow manage to keep them separate.

When it comes to learning to USE language, however, the results are more variable. If you haven't learned to USE language to do good small talk, it won't happen, not because of *who* you are, but simply because of *what you are not doing*.

Research shows that people who chat easily are systematic in their behaviour (whether they are aware of it or not). They listen in a particular way, they ask questions in a particular way, and they know what to do or say next because they have a sort of map in their minds of how they want the conversation to unfold.

Rate Your NetworkAbility

When you set about improving your skills in any area, it is enormously helpful to start by setting a baseline. This Personal Skills Checklist is helpful to enable you to tune in to both your strengths and the things you need to work on. Simply go through the questions and circle the answer you think most closely reflects your current capabilities.

	Strongly Disagree	Somewhat Disagree	Neutral	Somewhat Agree	Strongly Agree
1. I can develop a rapport with people even when there is not an immediate natural connection.	1	2	3	4	5
2. I can have a comfortable, relevant conversation with a new contact on a variety of social and business topics.	1	2	3	4	5
3. I can interest contacts in what I might offer; I can build their perception of value.	1	2	3	4	5
4. I can introduce the subject of business without being perceived as inappropriately pushy.	1	2	3	4	5
5. I can get into, and get out, of conversations comfortably.	1	2	3	4	5
6. I can ask relevant questions without appearing uninformed.	1	2	3	4	5
7. I am aware of the key frustrations clients face in various sectors and how I might help to address them.	1	2	3	4	5
8. I can find the personal motivation behind someone's overt business motivation.	1	2	3	4	5
9. I can rate the likely quality of a contact	1	2	3	4	5
10. I can value appropriately different types of contacts (e.g. potential new accounts, 'connectors' and influencers of decision makers).	1	2	3	4	5
11. I can purposefully build a business relationship over time, in order to gain referrals, information and work.	1	2	3	4	5
12. I am comfortable with interpersonal risk.	1	2	3	4	5

Most people don't get straight 5s when they first go through this, although it is a perfectly achievable target for anyone who sincerely puts the material in this book into practice.

A sensible starting goal is to pick the two or three questions which jump out to you the most, and resolve to improve your score by 1-2 points over the next three months. Calculating a numeric score can provide evidence of progress before you are producing tangible results such as desired sales or collaborations.

The Special Ingredient of NetworkAbility: Being Prepared to Take a Small Risk

A common question that arises with this questionnaire is: 'What do you mean by interpersonal risk in Question 12?' It's an important issue. Figure 3.2 below uses the same dimensions as Figure A1.1 in Appendix 1. In that Appendix we pointed out that as you get more commercial in your approach to your profession, you will need not only to maintain your concern for the tasks you do, but also to develop your concern for the relationships you have with business contacts.

You can certainly take the idea that relationships are important too far, and frankly we know of quite a few people who have brilliant contact lists but don't actually sell anything to anybody.

To borrow a phrase from the management theory of Blake and Mouton, these people are treating their networking like a Country Club – they are having a great time but nothing is getting done. Instead, a more appropriate metaphor is to be like a farmer. The farmer realises they are trying to get work done, but accepts that in order to do that, they have to work with the ecosystem: it's about striking the right balance between task and relationship.

Figure 3.2

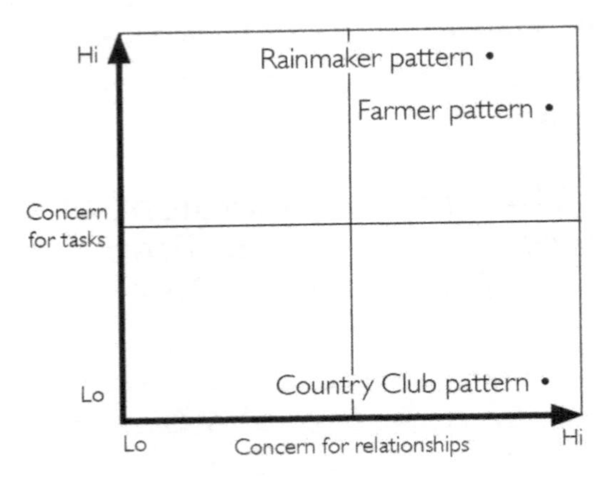

© Andy Bass 2005

So the farmer metaphor gives you a much better picture of what networking should really be like, but with one wrinkle that brings us back to interpersonal risk.

Research on sales teams done by Alan Weiss a few years ago looked at differences between average sales people and the real 'Rainmakers' – those who brought in disproportionate amounts of work to their businesses. Both groups were good at relationship building, but the Rainmakers had a clear distinction in their approach. When it came time to ask for something from the other person (a meeting, to look at a proposal, a sign-off on a new piece of work) the average sales person worried about negatively affecting the relationship if they seemed to show that they were only after something for themselves. This concern would inhibit them from asking for what they needed.

The Rainmaker was willing to ask the question, even if that felt like a risk to the relationship for the sake of the business. That's the willingness to risk that we are talking about in Question 12 and your willingness to go for it will make a big difference to your sales (and you should realise that the actually risk is infinitesimally small if you are offering the other person genuine value). Notice the position of Rainmaker on Figure 3.2 – that is the slight shift towards a concern for the task (as opposed to the relationship) that we are suggesting you need.

Final Thoughts

People often misunderstand how networking works to the point where it's hard to be effective. This book will make sure you understand networking properly so you will know why you are there, whether in fact you should be there, and specifically what to do before, during and, most importantly, after and on an ongoing basis.

Your own "NetworkAbility" is based on your current performance, an assessment of your skills and competence and more importantly your willingness to try new approaches in a series of controlled experiments over time.

Chapter 4

Location, Location, Location: Choosing Where to Network

We have already established that when time is a precious resource, you want to maximise the effect of any networking activity. This is particularly important if networking is not your favourite activity or if your opportunities to attend events outside working hours are restricted. If you are an employee in a large organisation, you may also want to think about the need to network internally, to find out more about different divisions or departments and to sources of information, contacts and possible mentors there.

Build Your Network Map And Find The Gaps

The next stage of the process is to collate all your current contacts and list them in one place. Take the various sources of information – business cards you have already, emails and contacts, address books on various devices and even scraps of paper and beermats – and put them into some searchable, comprehensive database. Use whatever works for you but ensure that you create a back-up at the same time. It is useful not just to have contact information but also to have the ability to categorise your network.

As we mentioned in the introduction a robust network has the following key components:

- Peers with whom you collaborate, share and seek inspiration.
- Mentors or potential mentors who guide your development.
- Mentees who will bring greater satisfaction and a younger perspective to your career.
- Clients and prospective clients (or employers and prospective employers).

- Multipliers – those who are not clients themselves but who can introduce you to number of clients.
- Champions or evangelists – those people who have used your services or products, or who have employed you and who will recommend you.

Look at the list that you have compiled: do you have plenty of contacts in some categories but relatively few in others? Do some people occupy two or more categories? We have found this to be a common situation with clients when they first map their network in this way.

Think of a network like a string bag – with each of the connections in it like a knot in that bag. A robust, well-rounded network can carry your career. There are no gaps or patches. Many people when they first do this exercise have a network that's more like a patchy spider's web: plenty of peers and clients for example, but few mentors or champions.

The point of this exercise is that, once you have ascertained where the gaps are in your network you can start to plan how you will fill them. The trick here is to identify the locations where the type of person you want to meet can most frequently be found.

It is amazing how many people think that networking does not get them the results that they want (new sales, job opportunities, a mentor etc) when they are in fact simply in a social setting with peers or friends and not in the locations where they are most likely to meet potential clients, employers or mentors.

The answer is simple. Pick your spots wisely. This chapter will help you evaluate the places both where you will feel comfortable and where there are people who are potential colleagues, collaborators, buyers and advocates. A trap for the unwary is to attend an event with a friend, stick to that friend all evening, lurking by the food table and speaking to noone and then to tell yourself you've been networking. You have not. The best you can call it is "going out" with a friend. Given that it takes time to develop a meaningful business relationships that produce results it is relatively easy to conceal such activity from colleagues and line managers.

This chapter looks at the most common places where business networking takes place:

- Business focussed and internal events
- Networking in other locations
- Dedicated networking groups, the sort that might immediately spring to mind when considering networking
- Social media opportunities for relationship development
- Networking opportunities at conferences and seminars.

Business Events And Internal Corporate Events

This section will deal with events that are targeted at your sector or profession. There are too many to mention individually but clearly they will fall into a number of categories:

- Events run by professional bodies, trade associations and unions
- Industry focussed networks
- Events run by your business such as away days or seminars
- Events run by business schools and academic institutions of relevance to your business
- Policy or politically focused events
- Awards events

A gathering of your peers is not necessarily going to be where you sell goods and services, but can be. As mentioned in the Introduction, there are many elements to a thriving network and it is not always about sales, but also about building an eco-system of contacts around you that will help you thrive in your business or your career. The conversation at events can deliver lots of "market intelligence" that larger companies pay high priced agencies to find out. Without specifically asking pointed questions about an individual's business needs, you can find out what the issues are in a given sector.

If, as an entrepreneur, you are a new entrant to the market with fresh ideas or an innovative product you may find older, more established businesses want to work with you to gain access to a market that is otherwise beyond their reach. A relatively junior employee can show initiative in finding out more about the sector or can meet potential mentors and experts at these events. There's no need to pretend that you are more experienced than you are: simply follow the conversational guidelines provided in Chapter 5 and you will soon be able to start and hold a conversation with anyone in the room regardless of rank.

Pick your event with care to get maximum impact for your time and cash investment. A free conference might have interesting content, but a day at a conference with a sizeable delegate fee may be a more savvy investment if it guarantees that you will be in a room with the people you really want to meet. For example: some film festivals attract a greater number of commissioning editors than others, some events include market places, pitching opportunities or workshops. The seminar on tax might seem dry or difficult but it could be a good place to benchmark your level of expertise.

The main difference in networking in your own sector or inside your own organisation is that you have the opportunity to contribute to the debates, questions and issues that affect your profession or business. Playing an authentic part in these debates, listening and contributing value can be an effective way to build reputation and profile.

Networking In Other Locations

So as long as you will be in the vicinity of the right types of contacts, you do not necessarily need to attend designated business networking events. This means that there are a much wider variety of locations and events that could become networking opportunities. These include

- Talks
- Workshops, seminars and training courses
- Showcases, gallery openings and cultural events
- Sports fixtures
- Activities you participate in on a voluntary basis
- Festivals
- Conferences
- Weddings and family events (clearly you need to be careful here – establish contact but save the shop talk for later!)

Anywhere it's comfortable and appropriate to talk. Expert networker Karl George often says, "If you don't go, you'll never know," and the trick here is to be a good guest, be open to developing the relationship and to simply making contact and following up with a more business-oriented conversation at a later date. Often very useful and interesting contacts are within your existing circle of acquaintances, but you may not have made the connection because of the context in which you know them.

One colleague got a major contract when she realised that she drove her son and a friend to football practice every other week and that friend's mother was the Managing Partner of a major professional firm in the city.

Conferences: Another way to display your business expertise is to run an event yourself or to volunteer to speak on a panel at a conference or symposium. Or to offer to moderate a panel if you think you have the skills. Alternatively, many sector organisations are run by voluntary committees and this form of voluntary work can clearly reap dividends in progressing your business or your career. They are often very time-consuming and hard work though, so again, consider your options and chose carefully.

Dedicated Networking Groups

What we mean by "dedicated networking groups" are those groups and organisations which are targeted at a range of businesses and which are set up solely or primarily for the purpose of fostering and nurturing business relationships. There are a large number of such groups to chose from. At first, you may simply wish to find out which organisations meet in your area. Typical business networking organisations include:

- Local or regional Chambers of Commerce
- The Institute of Directors (IoD) www.iod.com
- The Confederation of British Industry (CBI) www.cbi.org.uk
- Royal Society for the encouragement of Arts, Manufactures and Commerce (RSA) www.rsa.org
- The Federation of Small Businesses (FSB) www.fsb.org.uk
- Specialist networks focussing on industry sectors, professional qualification or regulation, geography or gender/race

- Informal local meet-ups and networks with minimal infrastructure

Fees vary widely. Some are free but a membership organisation can charge an annual subscription of £200 – £800 (depending on a variety of factors including your business situation and turnover). It will clearly be uneconomic to join all of them. The following steps will help you chose.

1. **Be clear about who you want to meet**. Is it peers or customers? Do you want to have a diverse group of business people in the group or would you be better with industry insiders? Do you want a local, regional, national or international reach? You may want to have a variety of targets which may require joining more than one network. You may also want to set a budget for membership of groups or discover which memberships (if any) your employer is willing to pay for.
2. **Be clear about why you want to meet them.** Are attendees going to be your future clients? Or can they introduce you to clients? Do you want to meet industry experts and possible mentors? Do you want a general picture of business prospects and opportunities in your area, or a more global overview? Are you interested in lobbying and changing policy in your sector or your area?
3. **Who recommended this to me and why?** Ensure that your friends and colleagues are not simply recommending a network because they feel safe and comfortable there. Will this network meet *your* identified needs? Some organisations, such as BNI, only allow one representative from each business to attend a given chapter, others, have a maximum number for membership per city. What are the implications of such restrictions?

4. **How does the network talk about itself.** Even just visiting the websites listed above can give you a flavour of the approach and style of the various organisations. For example 4networking.biz claims it is "50% business and 50% social and it works", the more sober CBI site speaks of its "unmatched influence with government".

5. **Are the events local to me at a time that works for me?** Be honest. If you are never going to be able to attend Breakfast Network meetings, whether because you have commitments that will not allow it or you simply are not a "morning person", then you may want to look at evening focussed events. If the events are more than a forty-five minute journey away will you genuinely make the effort at the end of a working day to travel?

Test out some events. Try before you buy. What is the conversation about in the meetings? Small talk is fine: as you will see later it is crucial in initiating and establishing relationships. But do you also get the sense that business is being done by these people (albeit not necessarily in the event itself.) Be clear and ask participants if they are getting the results you want by attending. Networking organisations will, in our experience, happily let you attend a couple of events to discover if it meets your needs. You may want to ask to attend at least two to test your first impression.

6. **Having attended an event, measure its effectiveness against your stated criteria.** Did you like the style of the event? BNI breakfasts, for example, are highly structured and more formal with a chance for everyone around the table to make a pitch or request, even guests. Other networks may simply rely on you all being in a room and present a relatively structure-free form of networking activity. Others again will

ring a bell every few minutes forcing those conversing to move on to a new person. Which was the most useful for your needs? Also review your criteria: does this network offer you something that you hadn't initially thought of? Also, how much will it cost to join this network? Not just in monetary terms, but in investment in time, effort and other resources. Then decide.

There is often a subtle interplay between cost and calibre of experience. For example, one of our associates who is a marketing consultant dedicates most of her networking budget to CBI membership because that forum puts her in the same room as directors of large corporations and government bodies: her key target list. At over £850 (with event costs on top of that), this consultant could join three or four, other, cheaper organisations but the CBI is pitched at the perfect level for the conversations she wants to have with potential clients. Consider a sharp-shooter rather than scatter gun approach: paying for one "perfect" membership and then filling the gaps in your networking efforts by finding other networking opportunities at low or no cost.

Social Media

Location is a more nebulous concept online. We refer to websites and networks as 'places' but the nature of the interaction often lacks the instant feedback loop that allows us to monitor the direction of the conversation.

Face-to-face in a given event (for example a talk at a CBI event by the governor of the Bank of England, a private view at a gallery or Friday night drinks for your team) you are all pretty much on the same page. Within a relatively small variation of needs and wants, you are all there for the same reason. You can tailor your conversation and there is sufficient commonality of interest and purpose in the context of the gathering to read the state of the person you are talking to. As you will see later – if a topic of conversation is not of interest you can ask a different set of questions to move the person you are speaking to into a more positive "state".

This is not as straightforward online. The internet allows conversations that are asynchronous: you can find a forum and post a comment weeks after the last comment was posted. You can see the Facebook status of a friend and 'like' it days after it was created. You can Skype call a potential business partner in California at no cost. You can enjoy some photographs shared on Flickr some months earlier. Connections can take place by bending time and space.

But the flip-side is that you might both also be in a very different 'emotional' place. Interacting online needs an understanding that nuances of mood can be lost, there's no tone of voice or body language to guide you.

In a 'busier' online environment you can react to someone's comment without knowing the context or back story.

Time spent on preparation and understanding the building blocks of relationship building can save you energy and effort.

- Take time to appreciate the etiquette and social rules of the online space you are entering just as if you were walking into a room full of strangers.
- Master the technology: use one or two sites well rather than everything badly. That said, use the syndication tools available

to publish the same content on a number of platforms to avoid duplicated effort.

- Give value to get value: just because it is as easy (almost) to send information to one hundred people as it is ten people, consider the relevance of what you are sending out. Again, a "sharp shooter" approach may be more fruitful in the long run than a spatter gun.
- Enjoy the time you spend online: if you do not enjoy communicating in this way, keep this part of your network building to a minimum.

Networking Internally

Some organisations have mechanisms to assist a newly arrived employee to get to know others in the organisation outside their immediate team. Social events, firm or company sports teams and leagues, trips to concerts, theatres and weekends are offered through social clubs and periodic firm-wide drinks are common. Through induction schemes and with internal mentoring or training schemes you can begin to build relationships with people outside your immediate department or team.

Other organisations may not emphasise that aspect of internal networking or may have divisions spread out nationally even globally. In these cases, the new employee may have to be more of a self-starter, but there are clear benefits to creating and disseminating your personal brand throughout the business you work in. This is particularly true if promotions are discussed across the business: when your promotion is being considered by senior managers outside your team, section or division, it will clearly be an advantage if they know who you are and have a good opinion of you.

What can an employee do to get to build a network in their own organisation?

Some juniors restrict their personal marketing efforts to their immediate boss or the person for whom they do most of their work. This can be a trap for the unwary if that boss or supervisor leaves the business or is reallocated to another team or office. The efforts have to start again from scratch. Ensure that your skills and efforts and your good results are shared with your wider team or department.

Offer to give training talks and write or contribute to an article if you can. If you chose your topic shrewdly, you can show your expertise off to your advantage.

When you first arrive at an organisation it is relatively easy to walk up to those you don't know and introduce yourself. But after that honeymoon period is over, keep going. It may feel very unnatural to say to someone, "Hello, you don't know me. I'm [name] and I work in [name]," when you have been in the job for a year or more, but it is never too late or too embarrassing to do so.

Whilst on the subject of embarasment: remember that you need to watch your alcohol intake at events. Copious amounts of (often) free alcohol may be available and everyone else may seemingly be throwing caution to the wind, but you may be mistaken. There is a thin line between being jolly and being embarrassing and you may not want to raise your profile for all the wrong reasons.

Other good reasons to get to know people outside your immediate department or team are so that you can find out more about the business and offer a more rounded appreciation of your own role and for you to find out about opportunities for progression elsewhere in the business. If you are stuck with a supervisor or boss with whom you have a poor relationship, finding a helpful mentor elsewhere in the business can allow you to reflect on how to improve your position or navigate the internal politics by having a fresh perspective.

Final Thoughts

We hope that this chapter has alerted you to the fact that developing your business network can, in some circumstances, take place almost anywhere. While business networks and professional or sector-led events are clearly designed for participants to network in a systematic fashion, you may feel more comfortable with a less structured approach. However, they are clearly an asset when your needs fit with the activities and constituencies on offer.

"The readiness is all," said Hamlet and while he was not talking about building a business network, he could have been. Your life will bring you in contact with a variety of situations and people and by keeping an open mind, being curious and willing to develop relationships you may find you have made a valuable business contact, regardless of the context in which you meet.

Networking is more enjoyable and effective when you find a way to do it that works for you. Then you will do more of it and you will more easily build a diverse network over time: which is really the name of the game.

So once you are clear on who you want to meet and why, you will have activated a personal radar that will help you spot such opportunities. This applies whether you are a business owner or an employee.

Now you are armed and ready: you have chosen the perfect networking location that meets your needs. You know that the people you want to meet will be there and you have a stack of business cards at the ready. You know and like the style of event and you are briefed about why you are going along. You know where you are going but not what you are going to do once you get there. And if you recall Chapter 3, you also know that your basic objective is simply to meet one or two interesting people, and get permission to re-contact them. The next step is to start talking to people – easier for some than others. So how do you kick off a conversation, approach a stranger and get to know them? Many people hate smalltalk, and they use the term as an insult. In fact some, especially the technically-minded, take the view that talking is purely for the transmission of data (and some of those are just saying that to rationalise the fact that they don't feel comfortable and don't know how to do it).

Chapter 5

Not So Small Smalltalk

In this chapter, we explain why you should give smalltalk more priority, and point out what you risk missing if you dismiss it too lightly.

The Power Of Smalltalk

Before we look at the skills of smalltalk, let's get things straight about its importance.

Smalltalk Is A Key Way To Build And Maintain Relationships

Anthropologist Gregory Bateson suggested that we can think about communication between people as taking place simultaneously on two levels. We'll call them the data level and the relationship level:

- Data level – the words spoken (the 'information')
- Relationship level – the context, including things such as voice tone, facial expressions and gestures (this level is where we negotiate our relationship to the other person)

The relationship portion of the message modifies the response to the information – it tells the listener how to interpret the message. This effect can be dramatic e.g. someone greets a friend by saying (with a broad grin), "How are you, you old s*d?" The words by themselves would be rude, but the way in which they are said conveys the message, "I like you; we are friends."

It's on that level that the relationship develops (and many people won't talk to you about business until they feel the relationship is appropriate). Making smalltalk is important because it is almost all about the relationship level – the 'information' can be quite trivial.

This may be a reason why some people find smalltalk hard. They ask themselves, "What am I going to talk about?" – their focus is in the wrong place (on the 'Data'). We will show you in precise terms where you should put your focus to have enjoyable and successful social (and social-business) conversations.

A Word About Body Language

We have mentioned that some of the relationship messages in a conversation get transmitted by non-verbal means: gestures, facial expressions and tone of voice. That leads to the whole question of body language. We looked into this in some detail a few years ago and here is our advice in brief: Don't even bother to think you can reliably read body language. Unless you are a highly trained interviewer or interrogator, it will probably because you more trouble than it will give you benefit. If you are preoccupied with trying to work out what someone is thinking, you will be guessing, and you will neglect to actually pay attention to them. Furthermore, you can change someone's body language through your communication with them, as we will see, so the value of whatever you read is dubious anyway.

A lot of the laboratory research that gets quoted in management training (like the old chestnut that "only 7% of communication is verbal") should have stayed in the lab – and the scientists who did it are sometimes surprised and concerned about the way their work is applied, in partially-understood form, by seminar leaders and amateur pop psychologists.

You should definitely pay attention to other people's non-verbal behaviour: are they attentive? Are they watching and listening? Are they animated, or low-energy and listless? But beyond these basics, a little knowledge is a dangerous thing, and there are better avenues to pursue for the typical person wanting to increase their business communication ability.

A Lot Of Business Gets Done During Smalltalk

What do managers really do? A lot of people have asked that question, but joking aside, Henry Mintzberg produced an answer that surprised a lot of people in the 1970s. He and his co-workers actually followed managers around all day to find out. They thought they'd find that managers are busy 'running the numbers', giving orders and going to formal meetings. To their surprise, and contrary to popular belief, they found that general managers spend most of their time in conversations, often on topics not directly related to the business, but nevertheless central to maintaining networks and relationships and to developing goals and action plans.

Furthermore, other academics following Mintzberg's style of work discovered that the most successful managers spend more time socializing and interacting with outsiders than did their less successful counterparts.

Helpful Attitudes

These are not 'the truth' for all time and all conversations. Consider the following points when making smalltalk with potential and existing contacts:

- **It's not about what you talk about.** Remember, smalltalk is about building relationships. Recognise that there are different kinds of conversation. If you just need to transmit data, use email. But recognise that it's much harder to build trust in such an impersonal medium.
- **The most interesting people are the most interested people.** This attitude is really helpful if you have trouble knowing what to say to someone, because instead of trying to wow them with your wit and wisdom, you can ask them questions and find out what you can discover. Many of the skills we cover in this book are therefore questioning skills.
- **People like to be put at ease.** In our own research and in our seminars, we are constantly surprised by the confident and successful people who tell us they find smalltalk difficult. Many people will be grateful to you if you cultivate the attitude that you will put them at their ease – as if you are secretly one of the hosts of the event. As you help them relax, you will find the experience more relaxing and comfortable yourself.
- **The other person wants the conversation to go well.** It's in their best interests, if you think about it. Many times we've been to both business networking and social events and cheerfully introduced ourselves to some blank-faced individual (it would be easy to describe them as looking unfriendly), only to receive a big smile and hear a relieved sigh in return. They've been rescued! You can be their rescuer.
- **You can lead a horse to water, but you can't make it drink.** It's helpful to recognise that the other person just might not want to talk. They may be painfully shy. They may have had a bad day. They may be preoccupied. Sometimes it's best just to move on. Funnily enough, it's not unusual to find that you meet them on another occasion and they behave quite differently.

- **Some people enjoy power-plays.** Unless you enjoy a challenge, or they are paying you enough to make it worthwhile, there is no obligation for you to put up with people playing power games, or to allow them the privilege of your company. We suggest you leave them to their antics and find some more agreeable conversation partners.
- **There is no "one right way" to chat.** As an illustration, consider the wide variety of popular and successful TV presenters and interviewers – they do not all fit into one style. Use the exercises provided in this book to develop your own style.
- **Confidence doesn't mean competence.** If you think you lack confidence, consider this: confidence is built on competence i.e. skill. Very often, 'nerves' or feelings of 'shyness' are just a signal that you are going into a situation for which you need extra skills. The great thing about skills is: you can learn them.

The main skills for effective conversation have to do with the directing of attention: a) yours and b) your conversation partners. And you will discover that, in essence, your attention should be on your partner, and theirs should be on you or, better yet, what you are talking about.

Removing Blocks

There are various mental blocks that get in the way of making enjoyable smalltalk easily. By recognising what may be getting in the way of your ability to make easy smalltalk with people, you can become a better conversationalist and networker.

Automatic Or Unconscious Rules Learned As Children

The pioneering family therapist Virginia Satir pointed out that, based on her extensive clinical experience, the strongest human drive is not towards life or sex or money, it's...

- The drive to do what is **FAMILIAR.**

The truth of this has dramatic effects, and if you think about it, you will find evidence to support it: people stay in marriages and other relationships that are effectively over, people stay in countries in which they are persecuted "because they've always lived there", and many people throughout history have preferred to die rather than allow their culture to change.

Where do these habitual patterns come from? Well, the words 'familiar' and 'family' have the same root. The things we learned as children may have been appropriate then, but as adults we have the choice to re-evaluate our rules.

Here are some of the rules people learn as children that relate to smalltalk:

- Don't talk to strangers
- Don't speak until spoken to
- It's 'rude' to be 'nosy'
- Don't talk about religion, sex or money
- Don't be 'pushy'

Now, a salesman with these beliefs is not going to do very well! And neither is a would-be conversationalist. While there were usually good intentions behind such rules, for example protection, acceptance (or just to avoid the embarrassment of parents!), as an adult, a person can choose to re-evaluate their worth. Some people may need to seek one-to-one help with this, but for most, a new look at an "old family movie" can bring the ability to make a new decision and shake off old limitations.

Ask yourself: What rules were you brought up with? Do any of them still affect you? Do you need them any more?

Questionable Beliefs About Power And Friendliness

Another area of blockage can come from questionable beliefs about power and friendliness. The two we hear most often are:

- It's better to be 'feared' (or 'respected') than 'liked'.
- To be perceived as 'friendly' is to be perceived as 'weak'.

Interestingly, animal behaviourists report that in monkey colonies, it is not the biggest, strongest monkey who is the leader; it's the one with the most friends.

The Belief That Smalltalk Is Trivial

We sometimes hear this belief expressed with a cynical tone of voice by intellectuals and techies in particular. We've already provided reasons why smalltalk is not trivial even if the 'data' is lightweight. When we dig a little deeper, what we usually find is that this attitude is a smokescreen. It masks something else: fear (for example fear of rejection or of appearing foolish).

Realistically, what is the alternative to small talk in this context? Enquiring after the pension provision, prostate or progesterone levels of a relative stranger is simply too much too soon. Smalltalk fulfils the function of making the other person feel safe and receptive to what you subsequently have to say. And, to quote the old Broadway number, "It's Not Where You Start, It's Where You Finish".

Anxiety

Here's a well-meaning suggestion you've no doubt heard: "Don't worry". There has never been a more useless or ineffective suggestion.

First, the very words raise the possibility that there is something to worry about. If we say, "Don't imagine your next-door neighbour naked", then that's exactly what you do think of (clearly this could be good or bad, depending on who lives next door). Similarly if someone says, "Don't worry", you have to think about worry in order to understand the very meaning of the words. Secondly, 'Don't worry' doesn't tell you what to do; it doesn't replace worry with something which works. And thirdly, implying that there is nothing to worry gives you a stick to beat yourself with if you are feeling that way ("Oh, I shouldn't feel worried but I do: what's wrong with me!").

So when someone (perhaps even yourself) tries to make you feel less nervous about networking, they may make the anxiety you feel worse.

Don't worry about worrying! If you feel worried about entering a social situation to chat, just take it as a signal that you may not yet have the skills needed to handle the situation. Treat it as a useful message, and decide to learn the skills in this guide and once and for all learn how to enjoy a conversation with someone new.

Using Smalltalk To Direct A Conversation

John Grinder, co-originator of NLP (an influential discipline concerned with effective communication) tells the following story:

John's daughter, at the age of about eight, asked him, "Daddy, what is NLP?" Rather than give her a technical explanation, John did something more practical: he gave her an experiment to try. He said: "Go and ask Grandma (who was in the next room): 'How's your arthritis today?'"

John's daughter went next door, and returned a few minutes later.

> *"Well," said John, "Did you ask her?"*
> *"Yes," replied his daughter.*
> *"What did she say?" asked John.*
> *"She said it was good of me to ask, but that it was really hurting."*
> *"And what did you notice: how did she sound?"*
> *"She scrunched up her face and sounded like she was in pain."*
> *"Go back and ask her this," said John. "Ask: Grandma, did Daddy ever do anything really funny when he was a little boy?"*
> *Again, John's daughter went next door, and returned a few minutes later, this time with a grin on her face. John grinned in response.*
> *"Well", said John, "Did you ask her?"*
> *"Yes," replied his daughter.*
> *"What did she say this time?" asked John.*

"She told me this really funny story about how silly you were when you were little, Daddy!" replied his daughter.
"And how did she look and sound this time?"
"Oh, she was laughing and she seemed happy."
"So, different from the first question?"
"Oh, yes, completely different."

This story has a profound lesson for a would-be conversationalist. Notice that the first question, "How's your arthritis today?" could be thought of as 'polite' or 'caring', but its results were pain and discomfort for the grandmother. The second question takes things in a new direction completely. It directs the old lady's attention to charming memories, and cheers her up. (Please note: we're not advocating ignoring peoples' suffering – just noticing to make sure we don't magnify it.)

A conversation is either stalled, or going somewhere. Everything you say affects which direction it's going in and is therefore a key thing to pay attention to. Instead of being self-conscious, be 'other-conscious'. Then you will discover something crucial: that, like John Grinder's daughter, your contributions to a conversation can influence its directions, so move it in either a pleasant or unpleasant one. Once you notice that, you can begin to choose a new direction that you and your conversation partner like.

How Questions Work

A good starting point is to consider how questions work. They don't just request data: *questions direct attention*. Where we put our attention influences how we think and feel about our experiences.

You can try this out on your own. For example, next time something doesn't go quite according to plan try asking yourself the question:

- "Why did I screw that up again?"

versus

- "What did I do right this time?"

and compare their impact. Take the time to answer and notice which one feels better. Few people ask themselves the second question, yet this habit speeds up learning like you wouldn't believe (we will return to the use of self-questioning to speed up your learning in Chapter 8). This goes for questions you ask other people too.

Exercise: Questioning with a direction in mind

Find someone to practice with – with their agreement – before you do this 'for real.' It's a conversation game where the object is to get your partner to feel as positive as possible just by asking questions with a positive direction in mind. How do you know what direction you're going in? By really listening and watching how your partner (P) responds – do they become more lively and animated (good) or unresponsive and turned off (bad)?

1. Ask P the routine question, "What kind of week have you been having?".
2. If P's answer is in the direction you want (positive and resourceful), ask for more and more detail to lead P towards a more and more positive state.
3. If the response is in a negative, flat or boring direction, try

out direction-changing questions such as, "What would be better?", or, "How would you prefer it?" etc. Once the direction changes, ask for more and more detail about the positive state.

4. Observe carefully and notice P's gestures, facial expressions (eyes, mouth shape, blushing etc), breathing (sighs etc).

This game develops key skills for building rapport, and for helping people feel good about themselves. Paying attention to the responses you are evoking makes a big difference to the outcomes of conversations, not to mention consultations, meetings, presentations etc. Notice, too, that this is what John Grinder was showing his daughter.

It often works well when looking for positive states/feelings to ask about the best experience of something, favourite times/places etc.

What kinds of experiences should you be asking about? Ideally ones about which the person feels:

- Curiosity
- Enthusiasm
- Learning
- Motivation
- Excitement

Let's consider some examples. First, let's look at a line of questioning which is going in an unhelpful direction

You: What kind of a week have you had?
Them: Oh, it's been pretty boring.
You: How come?

Them: Just work, you know…
You: Oh, what do you do?
Them: I'm a Project Manager.
You: Oh right.
Them: (Silence – looks a bit downcast)
You: (Silence – trying to think what to talk about now)

Comment: The mistake here was to ask the person what they do after they've just said that they find it boring. At this point you know very little about this person, but you can be sure that this is the last thing they want to talk about.

Here's another way this could have played out.

You: What kind of a week have you had?
Them: Oh, it's been pretty boring.
You: How come?
Them: Just work, you know.
You: Yeah… (Pause) So, have you got anything more interesting coming up?
Them: Yes, I can't wait for the weekend.
You: Why what have you got on?
Them: Oh, nothing in particular, just looking forward to chilling out and seeing my mates. Might watch the Grand Prix.
You: Oh right, are you a fan then?
Them: I am a bit, to be honest, yeah. (Smiles and looks enthusiastic)

Comment: The trick here is to leave the work topic well alone. They've said it's boring. So look for something, anything, that might be more interesting to them. In this case, it turns out to be the Grand Prix. It could have been shopping, clubbing, football, stamp collecting or parrot racing. The only thing that matters at this early stage is that the person you're talking to responds positively to the question.

We encourage you to practise this exercise a few times before moving on. Start with friends and family. Find out how it works, where it works and when it doesn't. Remember, it's a skill, so it you need to practise to get fully comfortable.

Other-Directed Communicating

For effective smalltalk use a basic *loop* that goes like this:

1. Start with a straightforward, unthreatening question such as: "What kind of a week are you having?"
2. Notice the direction of the response you get.
3. If you like the direction, ask for more details.
4. If you don't, ask a refocusing question, e.g. "What would you like instead?"
5. Go to 2.

Smalltalk Q&As

The following sections cover some of the questions we've been asked about smalltalk. Some of the questions were asked of us in a challenging manner – there can be a lot of emotion around when the stakes for getting the results seem high. We present the answers we gave, in the hope that they clarify the material

Q: Do you seriously expect me to think about all of this while I'm talking to some finance director at a dinner?

A: The answer is simple: Yes.

Q: Do you really mean that the main tactic for making conversation is asking how people's week went, and if they sound a little down about that, to follow up with, "How would you like it to have gone?" It doesn't seem that likely to work to me.

A: Well, I agree that if that is what we were suggesting, it would seem less than magical. But you may have missed our intention. The point is not the words you say themselves, but the actual response to them, which will be different for any person on any given day. It's this real-time response we are drawing your attention to.

The exercise called "Other-directed communicating" is a way of training yourself (therefore needs practice) to treat the response you get from the other person – what you see and hear in their non-verbal behaviour – as information about what direction to steer in next.

Our point is that even as mundane a question as "What kind of a week have you been having?" (or any other of a load of similar starter questions) is a perfectly good jumping off point, as long as you pay attention to the response, and track in the direction of the other person being animated and enthusiastic. Once they're talking about what they're interested in/enthusiastic about, you ask them more and more about it, and the smalltalk will flow.

It seems too simple, we know. This is a problem for us as workshop leaders – if smalltalk is such a big problem for people (and it often is), they expect the answer is going to have to be complex. All we can suggest is that you practise the exercise as laid out in the book and test it in the real world a number of times.

Q: I just can't see it working – can you convince me?

A: When someone says, "That would never work", our response is always, "Test it". They are using 'logic' (which may be based on flawed premises, after all) and we are encouraging controlled experiments.

Q: How will this make me seem witty or sophisticated?

A: We'd say it's a common mistake to think that smalltalk has to be witty or sophisticated. If you listen in to other people, and think about the way you chat to friends, the words are usually very mundane: "Oh yeah, that movie is really cool," etc. Smalltalk is not about delivering Shakespearean sonnets! What is key is the emotional tone – the mood music, not the words. (Remmeber, we're just talking about smalltalk here. Obviously in a negotiation, say, the words are very important – but that's another kind of communication).

Q: Surely what we need is not to learn how to tell whether people are interested, but to learn how to be interesting?

A: Well, consider this: that person you're meeting already has their interests. Given that there are so many weird and wonderful things that humans can get interested in, and how much tastes vary, how can you have a good chance of having something interesting to say to everyone you meet? The usual answer is to try to be a "renaissance" man or woman. But while the would-be renaissance man or woman is busy in their bedroom learning to be an all round street entertainer, musician, magician and stand-up comedian with an encyclopaedic knowledge of arts, sciences, humanities and current affairs, the competent smalltalker is out there asking people about their interests and noticing that the more you do this, the more people enjoy the conversation, and the more you learn from them. The weird thing is, they then think you're interesting automatically!

Final Thoughts

Once you start to notice how your communication is affecting the state the other person is in, smalltalk starts to get much easier. The trick is: Always aim to leave people in a better state than you found them.

While the techniques in the book are simple, they're also extremely effective. The magic of smalltalk is effective as long as it's implemented. It is simple, but not necessarily always easy to do unless you practise the skills. The formula is:

Practice → New Skills → New Actions → New Results

Chapter 6

Developing The Conversation: Further Tools And Tactics

In this chapter, we build on the knowledge you've gained in Chapter 5 and boost your networking ability with tools to enable you to keep the conversation going, learn more about the other person, and build the foundation of rapport that will support moving the conversation in the direction of business.

The Eliza Technique: Never Be Stuck For Something To Say

The ELIZA Technique takes its name from Joseph Weisenbaum's artificial intelligence computer program which used the same method so convincingly his secretary liked to discuss her problems with it because "it listened better than most humans". ELIZA worked by simply selecting some portion of what you had just said to it, and using the selected portion to build its next question. e.g.

They say: I like comedy clubs.
You say: Oh, Comedy clubs?
Or
They say: "We're going to the Cotswolds this weekend
You say: Oh, the Cotswolds?

You ask the question with a tone of voice which conveys the idea: "I've heard you. That's interesting. Tell me more." This simple strategy gives you a useful way of:

- Keeping a conversation going
- Keeping it relevant to the other person (because you are automatically following their train of thought)

As amazing as it seems, this simple device, combined with a sensitivity to direction, can keep a conversation going for ages.

Just repeating, with an interested tone of voice, the last important words someone said, is the simplest of the ELIZA patterns. There are many powerful enhancements to this basic idea, and we will have more to say about ELIZA patterns later on. But for now, do not let the simplicity of the basic idea fool you. This is an invaluable and incredibly effective tactic.

You don't do this ELIZA pattern all the time. With a little practice, you will quickly learn which are the best words and phrases to repeat in this way. And you will build the foundation for a whole raft of invaluable communication skills, including the next one: Discovering Hot Words…

Exploring And Using A Person's "Hot Words"

Have you ever noticed that when you get together with friends who share an interest you have, the conversation becomes animated, and as you reminisce about great experiences you've had, you start to feel that way now, in the present moment, too? What if you could encourage people to have the same feelings when they were talking with you, even if you knew nothing about the thing they were interested in? They would really enjoy the conversation, and you'd feel comfortable and have a good time too, wouldn't you?

Here's how to do it… People have 'hot words' which represent their values and criteria, and which have a lot of personal meaning for them. We can use these to enter into their world, build rapport and take the conversation in a promising direction.

Do the following exercise in a formal way until you get the idea. Once you get the idea, it is easy to have 'hot words' become a natural part of your conversational style.

1. **Ask about what kind of things a person enjoys.** They may answer about activities, things, places, information or people, for example.

2. **Ask, "What is important to you about that/them?"** Get a list of about three criteria. If they dry up, ask, "What else...?"

3. **Notice the exact words, tone of voice and gestures they use for each of their criteria**. E.g. they may value holidays which offer *sun*, *adventure* and *good food*. The words in italics are the 'hot words' that they use to stand for the criteria they most value.

4. **Check your understanding.** Say something like, "Okay, let me make sure I understand you..." Repeat the 'hot words' and phrases back as exactly as possible.

5. **Notice whether you get a congruent response or not.** If you do, you know what they will be motivated by. E.g. if you are recommending holiday destinations, you will get much more interest if you describe places as having *sun, adventure* and *good food*, rather than a hot climate, fun and tasty meals (even if those two lists may seem to be saying the same thing from your point of view).

If you're not interested in the topic they are talking about, become interested in how come they're interested.

Ask, "What's The Story Behind That?"

You have just read the single best conversational question we have ever found. And countless students and delegates have told us this question can have miraculous effects on the conversation.

Remember the basic ELIZA pattern, in which you repeat the last significant things they said using a curious tone of voice? Now, follow what they say with a deeper question (bear in mind the direction) e.g. Why? How does that work? What's important about that? What's the story behind that?

Use Softeners

Remember when we were talking about helpful attitudes in Chapter 5, we emphasised the need to put people at their ease? This is crucial. Remember: when you're asking questions, you need to be careful to avoid making them feel like they're being interrogated.

Now, this is easy if you keep watching the direction. Then, if you ask something that makes them uncomfortable, you'll notice and you can apologise and ask something else.

If you'd like to ask a question so as to get to know someone better, and you're not sure if they'll mind, then use a softener. e.g.

I hope you don't mind me asking, but I wondered...?

Just so I understand better, may I ask...?

Use Quotes Followed By, "What Do You Think?"

Follow what they say with "That reminds me of..." (quote a story, magazine article, something your friend told you...), then finish up with a question that invites them back in, such as: "What do you think?"

Remember to keep an eye on their interest level, to avoid the risk of becoming a bore: you're after subjects you both find interesting.

It's a good idea to collect conversational material such as articles and films you can discuss.

Make sure you have heard a news report or seen a newspaper. If you're in the corporate world, you need to know what deals are going on (at least scan the front page of the *Financial Times* or *Wall Street Journal*, or look at the business section on the BBC website).

Meeting Someone For The First Time

Remember, you can't depend on body language to tell you whether someone will welcome an approach (body language research confirms our inability to read minds from expressions and postures). You have to act first to find out.

It helps to have a routine e.g. at a networking meeting:

1. Tune your attention to the outside world
2. Get their attention
3. Firm (not like a vice) handshake and make eye contact. Say hello.

4. Introduce yourself, and pay attention as they respond
5. Comment about the situation and ask a question
6. Ask a follow-up question (ELIZA), or observation and question.

The Three Second Rule

Some people go to events and start a conversation inside their heads rather than with other people ("What am I going to talk about?", "Will they be interested?" etc). This kind of internal dialogue is very unhelpful, leads to unnecessary discomfort, and at its worst causes "paralysis by analysis".

Much better to follow the Three Second Rule. It's the same principle as tearing a plaster off quickly, or jumping into a swimming pool rather than taking ten minutes to edge down the ladder.

Quite simply: If you see someone standing on their own, or even a group that look open to new people joining in, introduce yourself with a solid handshake and a smile within three seconds of seeing them (i.e. before the internal dialogue takes hold).

Easy starter Questions

- How do you come to be here?
- Who do you know here?
- How do you know the host/hostess?

Easy follow up questions

- What do you do for fun?
- Anything interesting come up for you?

From then on, use ELIZA patterns (remember "What's the story behind that?") and the other tools you've developed.

Remember, in the early phases of a conversation it doesn't matter much what you talk about. What matters is the response of the other person. And the sort of response you want is of interest or enthusiasm. Since you don't know in advance what they will be interested in, you have to ask questions and notice the response (rather than having clever things to say, or offering them the dreaded 'elevator pitch').

Example Scenario

Here are three examples of smalltalk. In each case they start the same way – you ask someone if they've seen a film and they are rather blunt in return – but they continue very differently according to your responses. People are very varied in their likes and dislikes at this superficial level, so you will often be in a situation where you disagree in your opinion about things like films, clothes, holiday destinations, sports and pastimes.

You: I saw The Social Network this weekend, have you seen it?
Them: No – I hate all that Facebook stuff.
You: Oh, no really it's a brilliant metaphor for the fabric of modern society...blah, blah, post-modernism etc... (continued over-intellectual waffle)
Them: ZZzzzzzzzzzzz

Versus

You: I saw The Social Network this weekend, have you seen it?
Them: No – I hate all that Facebook stuff.

You: Oh, really, what kind of films do you like then?
Them: Romantic comedies.
You: Not that sentimental rubbish!
Them: (Silence)

Versus

You: I saw The Social Network this weekend, have you seen it?
Them: No – I hate all that Facebook stuff.
You: Oh, really, what kind of films do you like then?
Them: Romantic comedies.
You: Oh? Not really my thing. What is it that you like about them?
Them: Oh, I don't know really…
You: Well, what's your favourite?
Them: Oh I really enjoyed Love Actually.
You: Love Actually? What did you like about it?
Them: Oh it's really funny…etc etc (starts reliving the movie)

Final Thoughts

Over the last couple of chapters we have looked at the techniques which will get you into conversations with new people and help you keep them going. It's helpful to think about these techniques as being akin to the stabilisers on bicycles. They keep you upright so you can move forward, and they will keep you out of trouble in most situations, but they are not essential and can even feel restrictive. So if you find that you naturally click with the other person, then you can discard them.

A note of caution before you do, however. Almost everything we have looked at involves you asking questions and listening rather than talking. Remember what we said in Chapter 5: being really good at smalltalk is not just a matter of having 'the gift of the gab'. The best conversationalists are much more generous than that, and allow their conversation partners space to think and be heard.

Listening is vital because it is the only way you are going to learn something new. This will become increasingly important as we turn our attention to conversation about business.

Chapter 7

Knowing How to Move from Smalltalk to Business Talk

So far we have looked at practical ways to get into comfortable general conversations with new people, and we have pointed out that to start with, the mood music matters a lot more than the topic.

You will find that with some people, you have to make a lot of smalltalk before they will even consider discussing business. Others will want to get down to brass tacks straight away. There are cultural preferences too, and they can be hard to know in advance. Our job is to give you practical tools, so, once you have finished this chapter, we will make sure you know:

- How to move the conversation from social niceties to business issues.
- When to make the transition.
- How to develop the business theme so that the other person finds you credible as a business person.

Knowing Why Are You There

Over dinner a young professional was discussing the business development session and he drew an analogy with the world of football. He talked about someone considered by many to be the most skilful player in the English game, but who never quite turned his skill into results. He mentioned that since moving to his new club, this player has started to capitalise on his skills, because the manager has made one vital shift in his thinking: *the point is not to do with players using fancy techniques; the point is to score goals.* As we said loads of people go to networking events (and social functions for that matter) without any clear idea of why they are there. If you go to a networking event with the intention of selling something to a complete stranger then you are probably going to be disappointed. Similarly, if you think that going to lots of events and being a social butterfly is a serious contribution to business development, then you are going to be disappointed.

When you go to an event, your aim is to make contact with people with whom there is some potential, and gain agreement (and the necessary contact details) to follow up at some mutually convenient time.

What Do Business People Talk About?

Consultant and author Alan Weiss has helped many people running small businesses to sell to executives in major corporations. Alan places great emphasis on creating a 'peer to peer' relationship with those people with whom you want to do business.

'OK,' you might say, 'but what if that person is the CEO of a multibillion pound firm and I am not? How on earth can I get them to think of me as a peer?' The answer is to go beyond the titles and relate to them as another business person. (Actually, and to many peoples' initial surprise, you will often find that very senior people are much easier to relate to in this way than those who are in the middle but are trying to put on a front).

So if you are going to relate to them as business people, you need to know: 'What do business people talk about?'

They talk about:

1. their own businesses,
2. their industry and
3. the general business environment.

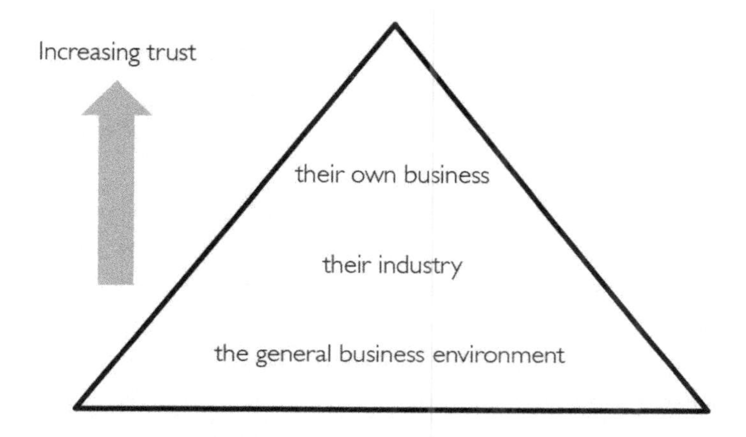

If they don't know you well, they might prefer to talk about the wider business environment before they let you into the world of their own business.

You can start to organise your own thinking about the general business environment the way a business strategy consultant might start working with a management team, with the simple mnemonic PESTLE (Political, Economic, Social, Technological, Legal and Environmental issues and trends). Just look how easily you can come up with interesting general questions using these headings:

- Political – How do you think public sector cuts will impact on your industry?
- Economic – I was reading that a lot of analysts expect interest rates to jump/plummet/ stay flat in the New Year – how will that affect your sector?
- Social – A lot of firms seem to be puzzled by how to manage digital native employees. What's your experience?
- Technological –What is the impact for your business of increasing smartphone usage/3D printing technology/ hydrogen based power?

- Legal – Do you think the law should be changed to make it more difficult for foreign firms to take over British ones?
- Environmental – is 'carbon neutral' just a marketing tagline, or do you think it has the potential to do anything worthwhile?

Have a go at generating similar questions for yourself. If you find it hard, take it as a sign that you need to beef up your awareness of current affairs. We often advise people to start reading the *Financial Times* and keep doing so until they can understand it (after which time they probably keep reading it anyway). You can do the same with the *Wall St Journal, The Economist, Forbes, BusinessWeek*, and the business pages of quality daily newspapers.

If you don't know about these things, you should learn. It's certainly not necessary to do an MBA, and there are a huge number of web and book resources out there. Here's a list of things you can work on to understand:

If you want to talk to senior business executives you ought to be conversant with the following concepts:

Central Bank Interest rate decisions (Bank of England, Federal Reserve, ECB and other important central banks)
Economic indicators: GDP/RPI/CPI
Some idea about current commodity prices (certainly Oil) and why they matter
Some idea about current exchange rates and why they matter
Market indices: FTSE 100, S&P 500, DJIA , CAC 40, DAX, Hang Seng, Kopsi etc – what are they?
Return on Investment, in general, and in the form of ratios such as

- ROA
- ROE
- ROCE

Stock market ratios: p/e ratio, eps, dividend yields
Financial reports:

- P&L
- Balance Sheet
- Cashflow Statement

Some well-known management models e.g.

- PESTLE (or PEST)
- Porter's Five Forces

Using A Map To Guide You To A Result

We introduced the idea of *direction* in a conversation early on, and it's crucial to success. In order to know what to say next, you need to know where you are in the conversation, and where you want to get to. The map below is designed to tell you just that. It is easy to remember and is very effective.

Fig. 7.1.The Conversation Map

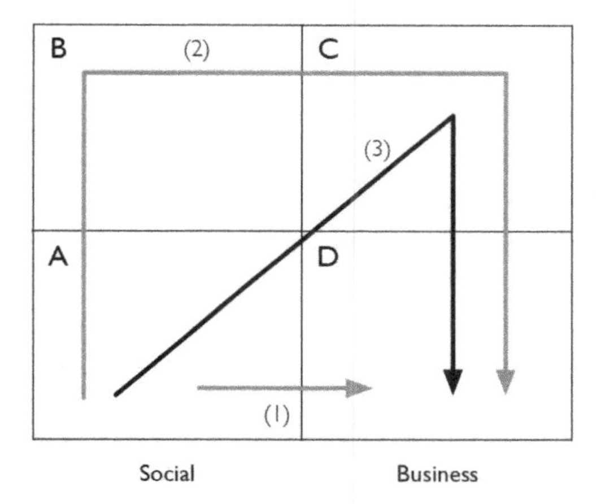

The Business Conversation Map™ divides the conversational game-board into four squares:

- **Social/Here-and-now.** This is chit-chat about the event, the speaker you just heard, the hosting organisation, the weather etc.
- **Social/General.** This is the topics you hear about when you do *Questioning with a direction in mind* – it can be about family, the weekend, hobbies, holidays etc. You can also use the "Hot Words" approach here (see the previous chapter) to draw the person out further.

- **Business/General.** This is where you discuss the general state of the business environment, the general state of the other person's industry, economic and political news, interest rates etc and how they affect the other person *in general*, or what their opinions are.
- **Business/Here-and-now.** This is when you are talking about a specific business issue of importance to the other person, perhaps one you can help with (or can refer someone to help with).

Refer back to the map. It shows three possible routes from social chit-chat to a conversation about a substantive issue.

- Route 1 – Usually too pushy
- Route 2 – A good general approach
- Route 3 – Often possible

The following bullets give some examples of questions and techniques you can use to move round from one square to the next. There are many ways to move from one quadrant to the next; here are a few that work well.

Often the transition will happen quite naturally, but if the transition is not natural, there is no need to rush. Don't try to transition until it feels comfortable. Remember, some people will be happy to talk business straightaway; others will be more comfortable on social topics while they get to know you.

A to B (social chat to build rapport): Questioning with a direction in mind: "How's your week been?", "Good weekend?" Ask for 'hot words' (what's important in an ideal X?) – holidays, hobbies, interests etc.

A or B, to C (general business): So, how's business? What do you see as the biggest issues facing your sector/industry/business? So what do you think about interest rates/the such-and-such takeover/etc.

C to D (get enough rapport, then look for reason for card swap): Is that affecting you very much? So what's the effect of that? Why is that important? Etc

We hope you can see that we have dealt with the A to B transition in Chapters 4 and 5, and that everything we have said so far in this chapter is about making the transition to Quadrant C. If this seems too overwhelming we suggest that you get really good at building Quadrant 3 conversations and everything else will fall into place.

Examples Of General B-To-C Questions:

- Any interesting new developments in the offing?
- What do you see as the current big issues in your industry?
- What are you working on at the moment that you're really interested in?

Developing Specific B → C Questions:

General questions are fine, but you will want to get more specific as soon as you can if you are to create any depth in the conversation. Here's a great exercise whenever you know in advance who you will be meeting (or at least can make an educated guess). Let's say you are going to an event where there will be a speaker about new developments in your city and how they will affect business. You expect that the sort of people you will meet will be:

- Partners in Big Four Accountancy firms
- Property lawyers
- Chief exec of a corporate division of a bank who has newly moved to the city
- The General manager of a large hotel that does a lot of conference business
- The Head of Planning at your local council
- The Managing Director of a local logistics company
- The finance director from an automotive company based on a local business park

For each of these people, what is the best B→C transition question you can come up with? Remember the PESTLE formula: Political, Economic, Social (in the sense of demographic), Technological, Legal and Environmental.

Once you ask your B→C question, keep the conversation going using ELIZA™ and "Hot Words" just as you did in Quadrant B.

C → D Questions Which Make Business Personal

- What's important about that from your point of view?
- So, what does that mean to you?

You can also (sensitively, with softeners if appropriate) ask for consequences to better understand their business needs:

- What are the most important knock-on effects of that as far as you're concerned?
- What is the ultimate benefit (or cost) of that (financial or otherwise) to you?

Taking It Further... New Location, New Time

Think about this statement: If you've met someone new and you've enjoyed talking with them, it's natural to want to talk some more. This is the key point of this section. It's easy to rush too quickly into asking for a further meeting, phone number, or to swap business cards. That's why working your way round the relevant conversation map is a good idea.

If you push it, it will often seem unnatural and uncomfortable, and so it won't happen, or you'll get someone's contact details because they are just being polite, and you'll find calls are not returned, people are always unavailable or in meetings.

We advise you to "Make Haste Slowly"!

Everyone Is Huddled Together In A Knot - How Do I Join A Group?

A lot of people worry about this – it's one of the most frequent questions that comes up in our seminars. Actually, it's almost a non-problem. A group will already be in conversation and it will often be difficult for them to include you even if they want to. However, look around – there will be others on their own, and it will be easier to start a conversation with them. They'll be grateful to be rescued (and we've met clients this way recently). If you do want to join a group, observe if they are in close rapport. If so, it's probably better to leave them to it. However, if they are standing in a way which is more open to the room, you can just ask, "May I join you?".

We can tell ourselves that "everyone" is already talking to someone and therefore fail to spot the person who is alone and open to conversation. As a test a consultant colleague of ours went to the opening of the offices of a city law firm and stood, perfectly alone in the middle of the reception. He waited and decided to note the time it took for someone to come and speak to him. Noone did. After forty-five minutes (he was testing the point after all), he simply left. For all anyone in that room knew, he was the CEO of a global corporation and a wealth of opportunity (not to mention goodwill) walked out the room with him. Anyone (from Senior Partner to summer intern) could have turned that situation around with a simple "Hello".

How Do I Leave A Conversation That Is Going Nowhere?

This is the second most frequently asked question. If the person you are speaking to is a client or customer of your firm, it's probably better not to risk offending them by leaving them high-and-dry: try and revive the conversation with one of the tactics we've taught you, and keep talking (or introduce them to someone else). Professor of Networking Julia Hobsbawm talks about "narrating your entry and your exit": there is nothing wrong with just excusing yourself politely – your time is valuable. If you're not sure if the event is worthwhile, you can always visit the cloakroom and reconsider whether to stay or do something else. And if you re-enter the event, you can then start a conversation with someone new.

How To Get A Business Card Or Other Contact Details

Some people seem to treat the exchange of business cards as a powerful ritual. In fact it's much easier if you regard swapping the card as a natural extension of the process of building a relationship – it's just the means by which you will be able to contact each other again later.

If you've been able to gather appropriate meaningful 'hot words', you've got a way to know if you can provide value (directly or by referral) and to demonstrate your understanding when you suggest taking things further.

Unless you've established a good reason for needing their details (ideally to enable you to provide some value for them), exhanging cards can be awkward and is unlikely to lead anywhere. With such a reason, however, getting a card becomes easy. At first, it can help to have something pre-prepared to say. Here's a template – modify it to suit your preferences:

If you've managed to identify something specific

"So if I understand, the issue you've got is <summarise key points arising from conversation>?" (yes). "Ok, well I think that's something we could talk about/I have contacts who might be able to help/I have an article (book) that could help. I'll send it you," (thanks) "Have you got a card?" (yes)

If you've not discovered a specific issue but the mood music is good

"Let's keep in touch, and maybe arrange a coffee or a chat on the phone." (yes) "Here's my card." They will generally give you their card in exchange).

Final Thoughts

- Have the attitude of a host. Leil Lowndes says that there are two kinds of people: those who enter a room and say, "Hey, Here I am!" and those who enter and say, "Ah, there you are!"
- Take your attention off yourself, and put it on the person you're speaking to. Remember to be other-conscious. If you're not interested in what they're interested in, become interested in how come they're interested. Who knows, maybe they're on to something.
- Keep an eye (and an ear) on the direction you're going. The answer to the question "What should I say?" is not in your head (so there's no point asking yourself!). A better question is "What seems to interest them?" or "What direction is this moving in?"
- Take an interest while avoiding an interrogation. Use softeners. Try, "May I ask you something I've been wondering about?" and, "Just for clarification, could I ask...")

Okay. So now you've finally got permission to contact.

Now what? The next step is vital: you must follow up on your promise, and fast.

Chapter 8

Now the Real Networking Begins

As mentioned above, networking begins after you have obtained permission to contact and swapped contact details.

This chapter will look at a number of approaches to reliable and effective follow up and will have a few "pipeline busters" for the times that your approach has stalled or seems ineffective.

The Fast Follow-Up

Fast and effective follow-up from an initial exchange of information distinguishes those with true NetworkAbility. Having invested in the initial work of making a new contact, make sure you reap the dividend by following up in a proactive and responsive way. These are the actions that will allow you to make the transition from an initial meeting to a business relationship.

If you have carried out your networking effectively you will now have a number of business cards and contact details together with some notes or reminders of the follow up actions that are required. This is where you may be very grateful that you made such notes as it can be hard to differentiate one person's card from another when their owners are no longer in front of you.

From Unconsciously Unskilled To Unconsciously Skilled

Some of the information in this chapter relies on a systematic approach to appraisal and evaluation which may seem artificial. We would say that these exercises are not artificial: rather they are conscious. The process of assessment and measurement set out in the following chapters are designed to move you along a learning curve from consciously unskilled to unconsciously skilled.

This refers to a theory of learning known as the four stages of learning devised by Noel Burch, employee of Gordon Training International. This describes the process of learning something new which may be familiar to you. The four stages are:

1. Unconsciously unskilled (You are not even aware that you have a learning need.)
2. Consciously Unskilled (You start to learn a skill and at this point realise that there is much to learn or fear that your income or self-worth will be affected if you do not learn the required skill. It is at this point where many people give up as their results are less than hoped for.)
3. Consciously Skilled (The learning has begun and the pain of learning has faded. You can carry out the required skill but are conscious of the learning process.)
4. Unconsciously Skilled (You are now so skilled that you operate instinctively and have absorbed the lessons of the past).

As someone new to networking, at stage two of the cycle, the act of focusing on positive outcomes and successes, however small, will inspire you to be persistent and let you see, as soon as possible, that you have arrived at stage three of the cycle. The transition to stage four is somewhat more subtle – often you will be proficient for some time before realising that you are effortlessly growing and maintaining your network.

The route to unconscious competence begins with a single step: in this case the execution of some follow up actions to build on the great start you have made.

Log Your Data

Take the business cards, contact details and even beer-mats or napkins you have collected and put them on your database. Depending on your situation this may entail a specific protocol around corporate Customer Relation Management (CRM) records, a spreadsheet or a smartphone app that you maintain yourself.

For the growing business, a well stocked and up to date database may well end up being one of your most valuable assets so it's a good investment of time and energy. Get as much information, as fully as you can and organise it so that it is searchable.

The mechanics of the system are not as important as having a system in the first place. Research on "rainmakers" (those who consistently and successfully bring in new business deals) shows that what sets them apart from other (lower performing) sales people is that they have a system and execute that system rigorously. One highly successful business director simply keeps all his business cards in a shoe box. Every six months he books a week out from his other duties and systematically calls every person for whom he has a card. He calls to see how they are and if they have any requirements. If they do he will book an appointment to see them in the following weeks. He books his diary up for the subsequent six months until the next review.

It is a very low-tech solution but what makes the solution so effective is not its technical sophistication but the regularity and consistency with which the director applies it.

Send An Email That Adds Value

You need to follow up on any agreed actions. Send the link to the article, blog post or website you recommended, set up the meeting, introduce the person of mutual interest. Within a few days (social), and on the same day or next morning (business), drop the new contact a quick e-mail along the lines set out below, and you're up and running.

If sending an article or piece of requested information, it is particularly useful if you (or your firm) wrote the article, briefing note, blog post or video link. Such a resource could be a highly useful piece of intelligence to share in the right circumstances. Sending technical or sector/business relevant information is a way of subtly sharing your expertise. If there is not a relevant technical article or resource to share, we feel that it is better to have some contact quickly than to allow a contact to cool off while you wait to find the perfect technical article or resource. The information that you pass on could just as easily be a great restaurant, a reliable electrician or relevant travel tip. As long as the intelligence you pass on has some element of quality and directly relates to an aspect of the conversation that you had, it will have had the desired effect.

If you spoke with your new contact about meeting up in order to talk further, then arrange the coffee date or lunch or issue the invitation that you said that you would. The communication does not have to be wordy or fancy. Something like this is perfectly acceptable.

Dear X,

Good to meet you today/at (event). I thought the attached document/link/item would be of interest/I have some contacts who could be useful/I have some ideas on (X,

Y). How about a phone chat/coffee sometime next week? Tuesdays are generally good for me.

Kind Regards,
[Name]

Assesssing Contact Quality

At some point you may meet more people than can be effectively held in a networking relationship. There are a variety of theories as to how many people that might be: "Dunbar's number" of people with whom you can maintain stable social relationships is 150. Regardless of the theory or an absolute number, within the time you have available to grow and develop relationships, to paraphrase Orwell, "All animals are equal, but some animals are more equal than others".

There will be some contacts that you will want to spend more time on as they represent key targets for you. In developing a network of contacts, *quality trumps quantity*. Here's a way of quickly prioritising prospective clients.

Fig 8.1 Quality Assessment

Quick Quality Scale (discuss and adapt for your situation)

Decision Maker: Can this person write or order a cheque/say yes to your project on their own authority?

No 0 1 2 3 4 5 Yes

Influential: Can this person introduce you to other networking targets?

No 0 1 2 3 4 5 Yes

Profitability: Is there an opportunity to develop high margin/high leverage/strategically important work with this person?

No 0 1 2 3 4 5 Very Much

Strategic alignment: Would this contact contribute to the value/brand/the strategy of the firm/practice group?

No 0 1 2 3 4 5 Very Much

Long-term value: Is there potential for a relationship of high future value?

No 0 1 2 3 4 5 Very Much

Revenue: If a potential client, is there the opportunity to charge a high fee?

No 0 1 2 3 4 5 Very Much

Cashflow: If a potential client, will they be likely to pay quickly?

No 0 1 2 3 4 5 Very Much

Consider Further Possible Follow-Ups

Now that you have made the first step, you can consider how you could follow-up and build the relationship. The mantra at this stage is "Give Value to Get Value". What value can you add to the relationship? Take a moment to speculate on the resources, contacts, information or ideas that might forward the relationship.

With a new contact you could plan where you might meet again and what you want to achieve from the relationship. Is this a potential new client or a peer? A champion or a multiplier? Could this person introduce you, when the time is right, to someone else on your target list?

You can also note what further research you need to do in order to get the most out of this relationship. Visit the company website, search to see if the company has been in the news or has any new developments. Notice whether your new contact has any particular interests, positions in the community or areas of expertise. Take an interest and seek out further points of common concern. The fruits of this research may lead you to believe that right now there is no further dedicated action to be taken. Some prospects are warmer or more relevant than others.

In the early stages it may be premature to make such a decision so be ready to find out more and get to know a contact in more depth rather than dismiss anyone out of hand. Growing a network is like gardening in this respect. Consider each of the contacts you make as a seed sown in the ground. When you have planted seeds, you do not dig them up a day or two later to see if they have grown. Seeds take root and germinate at their own pace. So do contacts in your network. Sometimes the 'reason' you have met someone does not become apparent for years. Sometimes you can pursue a key target for many months before seeing any real progress. As with the cultivation of a varied and self-sustaining ecosystem or garden: your patience will ultimately be rewarded, but *persistence* is the watchword.

Review Progress Against Your Marketing Targets

You can also evaluate what actions you might take on future in a similar situation. First, think about the event itself. If it is your first time at a particular event, was it useful and is it somewhere you might visit again? Did it meet the criteria you identified in Chapter 3? If you visited a regular engagement does it continue to meet your needs: there is a balance between familiarity and depth of relationship against a certain cosiness and "country club" mentality. ("Country club" as mentioned in Chapter 3 is a term coined by Blake and Mouton to describe the situation where everyone is having a good time but no business gets done.) Do you need to research some fresh networking opportunities?

Now consider the bigger picture. See how you have developed a relationship with your contact. Are you closer to making the sale or referral that you want? In Chapter 9 you will learn about the specific steps and tactics that you will need to create in order to move your contacts along a continuum. This process starts at their being contacts who know who you are, to clients who pay for your services, to champions who advocate on your behalf to others (or for those who will not become clients to multipliers who will find clients for you).

You may find it more useful to plan your sales pipeline and progress at quarterly intervals once your network is more established. In the early stages a more frequent review is useful in order to create a sense of momentum.

Take A Moment To Assess Your Own Performance

If you are new to networking and want to build your confidence and ability it is important to consciously review your competence and plan how you will improve. Remember, in learning skills, you get more of what you focus on, so accentuate the positives. We encourage coaching clients to keep a journal in which they ask the following questions after key events. Documenting your progress in this way creates a rewarding sense of progress and learning. Ask yourself these questions:

1. **What did I do RIGHT?** Make a mental, or better still, physical list. Was there a particular aspect of your skills that you wanted to develop and that went well? Did you get to speak to a person who has been on your target list and do you have permission to contact. Did you get to know some new people or re-inforce and build some existing relationships. Do you have a number of follow up actions and promising leads? Did you meet any particular challenge that you had set yourself?
2. **What did I do better this time than last time?** This allows you to compare yourself to previous performances and mark progress. These positive comparisons build confidence and ability.

3. **What skills to I want to improve for next time?** Which conversations could I have managed or handled differently? Which events might I attend in the next month or quarter?

Final thoughts

A client recently expressed surprise that we were going to have a half day session on Networking: "It's just going to an event and swapping business cards," he said, "how can we need four hours to learn about that?" After seeing the whole process and understanding the need for follow up, his tone had changed. When asked what he would like to stop, do differently or start as a result of the session he said: "I am going to start networking. I mean do it properly. I can see now that meeting someone is only the beginning."

During your 70 day programme you will be encouraged to stop and assess your progress from time to time: updating your records, reviewing your conversational and listening skills, mapping your progress along the pipeline are all activities that encourage learning. If you work the steps of the programme systematically you will quickly move from unconsciously unskilled to unconsciously skilled – in other words – to networking as a natural part of your working life (and hopefully an enjoyable and rewarding part).

The next steps are more like gardening: having planted the seeds of your network and given them the best possible start Chapter 9 gives you the tools to nurture your network and allow it to flourish.

Chapter 9

Nurturing Your Network – Creating Real Value

If you wish to be comfortable in any networking situation it helps to have a firm idea of the ways in which you add value to your network, your organisation, your sector or the cause you are working towards. This does not always have to be high-level technical knowledge or insight.

This chapter will help you recognise whether you have the potential to be a maven (an influencer), a connector or broker, a mentor or a mentee or an evangelist. If you build your expertise in one of these roles you develop a reputation amongst existing contacts and new contacts may be more amenable to meeting with you and getting to know you.

You can play these roles regardless of your age or status in an organisation or group. You may find that you are naturally drawn to certain roles, that they suit your personality.

As your network matures, as you become 'unconsciously skilled' in networking, this behaviour means that your network develops as other people seek you out or introduce you to new contacts. This has the additional benefit that you may not have to attend as many events (but you cannot drop out of the scene altogether) while still developing your contacts.

So now your network is established, this chapter will give you some ideas of how to you maintain and improve the landscape of your network over time.

Choosing Your Role In A Network

As mentioned above, networks benefit from a diverse range of people who carry out a range of functions within the group. The following is a non-exhaustive list of the types of roles you can fulfil:

The Maven (an influencer)

This term became more popular when Malcolm Gladwell used the term in *The Tipping Point* (Little Brown, 2000) for the type of person who is first to spot and adopt new or emerging trends. Having spotted it, they are very likely to broadcast their enthusiasm for the idea. *Mavens* are "information specialists", or "people we rely upon to connect us with new information."

They accumulate knowledge, especially about themarketplace, and know how to share it with others. According to Gladwell, Mavens start "word-of-mouth epidemics"due to their knowledge, social skills, and ability to communicate. As Malcolm Gladwell states, "Mavens are really information brokers, sharing and trading what they know". The Maven is useful in a network because they keep everyone up to date with latest innovation and developments. This type of activity can be time consuming so speaking to them (for example, about what smartphone you should select) may save you hours of research and comparative data.

The Connector or Broker

The 'Connector' is another term coined by Gladwell in *The Tipping Point*. A Connector has a wide and diverse sphere of more casual acquaintances and is trusted across the social boundaries and various groups found in the Connector's network. Whether by means of location, inclination or hard work, a Connector can put a range of people and ideas together. When working in combination with a Maven, they have particular strength and ability to bring new ideas and products to the attention of many people. It is the combined activity of the Maven and the Connector that Gladwell suggests will cause an idea to 'tip', to become widespread or mainstream. This is because the breadth of connections and the level of trust enjoyed by the Connector ensures that the idea is adopted across the board.

Being a Connector is a very generous act: it involves giving ideas and contacts away because the Connector can see that this is the way to move an idea forward. Connectors often derive pleasure and satisfaction from match-making in this way. If you speak to someone who says. 'If you want to do x then you should really meet y, they have been working in this field for years', then that is the Connector at work. Gladwell attributes the social success of Connectors to the fact that "their ability to span many different worlds is a function of something intrinsic to their personality, some combination of curiosity, self-confidence, sociability, and energy".

If you want to be further persuaded of the value of giving, connecting and brokerage in your networking activity you can also read *Give and Take* by Adam Grant, based on research on Givers, Takers and Matchers which hypothesises that, as long as they don't burn out "Givers" enjoy greater long term business and personal success than their taking and matching peers.

The extreme version of this behaviour is the person who says they know lots of people but never follow through or who trades introductions like favours, Mafia-style. Connectors have a hugely beneficial role to play in a network because they will grow your network for you, recommending you even when you are not there and brokering introductions and new contacts for you.

An Evangelist Or Champion

This person will similarly grow your network, but this is likely to be because of a specific relationship that the evangelist has with you, as opposed to with a range of people or types of people. Evangelists or Champions are people who praise you and then sell you and your ideas to others. They will do so primarily because you have given them great service in the past. That can be as a client or simply as a fellow member of your mutual network. Perhaps you introduced them to someone who subsequently became a valuable client or collaborator.

The absolute best way to create an evangelist or champion is to deliver them value. There is no guarantee that you will create Evangelists or Champions, but the word of mouth endorsement generated by a well placed Champion is particularly powerful marketing.

The best way to achieve that is simply to deliver value wherever possible and to reward or acknowledge authentically any endorsement or assistance. Champions and Evangelists are of supreme importance to a business or career. When seeking to reward or thank them, be creative and imaginative: provide an experience or gift that money can't buy that reflects your interests and talents in order to share your appreciation. A rich or powerful person may like a bottle of champagne or fine red wine but may love an artwork, invitation to an event or a book that they might otherwise never experience.

The Multiplier

A Multiplier, as the name suggests, is someone who is not personally a client or potential client, but who knows a lot of clients or potential clients. This could be because they share the same client group, often in a complimentary, but distinct, area of business. Thus law firms with corporate expertise in mergers will seek out partners from accountancy firms dealing in large corporate acquisitions, or IP lawyers put on events for patent agents. The accountant or patent agent in these examples will be working with a variety of businesses who are most likely to be the law firm's marketing targets. The value of the Multiplier is therefore clear: they will speak to your target market. Having profile and a good reputation amongst multipliers is likely to lead to introductions and recommendations.

Unlike the Champion, the Multiplier may be bound by professional ethics or other concerns and may not be able to endorse your services. However it is still important to have visibility with a Multiplier so that your name is 'top of mind' when seeking contacts or recommendations.

The Mentor Or A Mentee

Your network is a great place to find a mentor or to pass your expertise on to someone who is seeking to be your mentee. Mentoring is not coaching: the relationship usually takes place between an older, more experienced person who passes on the benefit of their experience and wisdom someone younger with less experience. You can benefit from mentorship at any stage of your career: newly appointed Managing Directors can get help on making the transition to the top post just usefully as a new trainee can pick up tips for negotiating the office from a recently qualified professional in the same firm. It is often interesting to pick a mentor who is in a related but different field: their perspective can be refreshing and can allow you to benchmark your practice or expertise in a wider context. If you are inspired to find a mentor, see the shaded box below.

Exercise: Finding A Mentor

Think about getting a mentor to help guide you in clarifying and achieving your goals. We are often asked about who you should pick and how you should conduct the relationship.

Who should you ask?

Ask the person who can give you guidance, who's done what you want to do. If you want to do something that's never been done before – chose someone who has done the equivalent of what you want to do in another sector or another sphere. Be ambitious. Ask the person you really admire and who you think will say no to you. The one who makes you think – "Well I'd love to work with them, but they'll never say yes". That's the person to ask.

That said, also seek to have some sort of relevance or personal connection. Cheryl Sandberg in her book *Lean In* has noticed that some women routinely ask her to be her mentor for no other reason than that she is famous and powerful. She likens it to the children's book *Are you my Mother?* where the hatching bird, estranged from her mother asks the eponymous question to a dog, a kitten and then in desperation a car, a boat and a plane. When the mother bird finally re-appears, the baby bird doesn't have to ask. He just knows.

She advocates being exceptional, having talent and then seeking out a person who would be motivated to encourage that talent by being your mentor. It's true that talent is very attractive to the potential mentor – so take some time to think about why you are asking that particular person rather than simply making a generic or anonymous request.

The person I want to ask is famous/ world-class/ out of my league/very busy/very scary

Ask them anyway. Be polite and specific and make a respectful request. In writing is probably best, but do not be afraid to follow up with a phone call if you don't hear after a couple of weeks. They may say "no" anyway but at least it is a sign that you are taking your own ambitions seriously. How are you going to get hold of these people? Think creatively about people you know who might have useful contacts. Thinking how you can use the "six degrees of separation" to your advantage to contact a potential mentor is good practice for creative problem-solving about how you will build a network for you and your business.

What should I ask for?

Be specific. Outline the reasons you have chosen your target mentor, reveal any relevant research you've done and give them an idea of the areas you'd like to discuss with them. If they say yes, then set up an initial meeting to make sure you will be compatible. If they say no, for example because they are too busy, find out if just a one-off meeting for coffee or lunch is a possibility. Don't take the rejection personally: time is precious and successful people are very busy and get many demands on their time.

The relationship can be what you want it to be but there are a couple of things to get sorted at an initial meeting – as well as giving your mentor some additional background and context to your work and what you want.

1. Agree the duration of the relationship and what form it will take – a meeting over coffee every six weeks – or dinner every month – or more or less frequently.
2. Chose a fixed commitment of six months or a year (or again, whatever works, but make it finite with an option to re-think, re-new and re-commit).
3. Identify a specific issue to address – or questions to look at so that your conversations are not too nebulous.

1. How will you do this – will you be more formal, with agendas etc or informal – or simply reacting to whatever is happening at the time.
2. Do you want to have specific topics to prepare between sessions or just use the session to take stock periodically and allow someone else to give you their impressions and an overview?
3. As the mentee, you may have to make an effort to fit in with your mentor's schedule

Any ground rules?

We think confidentiality is a given, but you can also think about how you will both show your respective commitments to the process by keeping to agreements, being open, listening and reflecting and respecting one anothers' time.

Keeping Track Of Where You Are With Each Person

If relationship-building is a step-by-step process, it helps to have a way of knowing where you are with each contact. Then you know what would represent a useful progression in your relationship. As an example, we have found the Lean Marketing Pipeline approach very effective (see Figure 9.1). You can view it almost like a board-game in which the other party moves through a series of stages:

- Complete stranger
- Knows who you are
- Networks with you, experiences your work (or otherwise receives some value)
- Becomes a customer or client
- Becomes an evangelist

And so on.

For each step, you decide what your 'Most Wanted Response' (MWR in the diagram), and what tactics you might employ (invitations to seminars, for coffee, sending articles etc).

Stranger	Knows Who You Are	Actively Networks with you	Is a Potential Client	Has Paid for work	Repeat Client	Network Multiplier	Champion
Wanted: Permisson to contact them. Their business card.	Wanted: Will give you time for a quick meeting. Will take a call	Wanted: Will seriously consider a specfic proposal	Wanted:	Wanted:	Wanted:	Wanted:	Wanted:
Requires: Has a positive impression	Requires: Is open to finding out more about your work	Requires: They recognise your potential value to them and/or thier contacts	Requires: They recognise a specific, currently relevant value you offer.	Requires:	Requires:	Requires:	Requires:
Tatics:	Tactics:	Tactics	Tactics:	Tactics	Tactics	Tactics:	Tactics

FREE → FEE

Fig. 9.1 Lean Marketing Pipeline ™
Lean Marketing Pipeline™. © Debbie Jenkins & Joe Gregory (2003).

The labels can be changed to suit your business, and other formats can be used – the key is to have a way of keeping track, and a prompt as to the next step to take with each person, based on where you are up to with them. To find out more about the Pipeline Approach, read *The Gorillas Want Bananas*, by Debbie Jenkins & Joe Gregory (2003), published by www.bookshaker.com.

Engage In A Step-By-Step Exchange Of Increasing Values

Be flexible in thinking about what you can exchange

Good negotiators are very creative in thinking about value – sometimes the other party is very excited about getting something you had overlooked as being scarcely worth anything, and you can gain a lot (by your own standards) at low cost to you and high satisfaction to them. Like a good negotiator, think very broadly about what might be valuable to a new contact – it certainly doesn't have to be business or even a referral to take one of the early steps. If they are a potential client, for example, you could be giving them new perspectives, the benefit of intelligent questioning, an opportunity to do some informal benchmarking, a chance to step back and reflect on their business. Sometimes you can add value just by the calibre of questions that you have asked or the perspective you have cast on that person's current business.

Saw This And Thought Of You (Give Value To Get Value)

There are many ways to maintain relationships with your network. In these days of digital connectivity, do not underestimate the power of a quick hand-written note. Rip out a newspaper or magazine article of particular interest to one of your contacts and send it to them. The article might just as easily relate to a recent conversation as to business matters. A restaurant recommendation or gallery review for an upcoming holiday destination that they mentioned. Or some insight into a business challenge they have talked about.

It's very low tech. Include a compliment slip or post it, with a quick "saw this and thought of you" type message and get it in the post.

Our colleague and master networker Karl George says that networking is like planting little seeds. You don't plant a seed and dig it up three days later to see how it's getting on. You just let it develop.

You do not have to follow-up in any major way, it's just a thoughtful gesture. But in doing so, you are demonstrating that you listen and that you add value. It's a good reputation to cultivate.

Give Value To Get Value - Online

It is this step, perhaps more than any other, that digital technology allows you to do quickly and effortlessly; on the fly, as it were.

E-mail, blog posts and some social networking platforms make sending ideas, images and information to specifically targeted people very straightforward. A quick personalised message with an image, weblink or pdf attachment which is highly targeted and tailored (in other words, which is "spot on" and timely) can be sent with a flick of the wrist or a few clicks of the mouse. However, in these days of email saturation and the relative scarcity of time and attention discussed earlier, this is still a tactic to use judiciously. Season your communication with such messages rather than bombard your targets with relative trivia.

The virtual networker has a number of assets to exploit at a tactical level to help develop relationships. Here are a few ideas to get you started.

- If you meet someone with a specific concern and you have some useful information to share that you have found online, send a link and a quick message when you follow up. This could be a judgment on the VAT treatment of Jaffa cakes, to the name of a great plumber in your area.
- This type of information has even more potency if it is a blog post or article that you have written. Not everyone can write in "mainstream" media (but if you can write for specialist press, so much the better), but we can all publish now.
- Some people have useful information available on their LinkedIn profile, which in itself provides a reason for people to contact them and for relationships to develop. Wayne Breitbarth's book *The Power Formula for LinkedIn Success* describes how Wayne, the owner of an office furniture company, has a "Office relocation checklist" available for download on his company's LinkedIn page. It is a genuinely useful and comprehensive document that discusses all aspects of office relocation and not simply furniture removal. But once someone has downloaded it, Wayne is entitled to follow up with some interesting (and potentially value-adding) questions of his own. This bullet point somewhat over-simplifies but ultimately Wayne is able to ask a couple of key questions "What size and type of office relocation is it?" and more tellingly, can he help by supplying them some new office furniture?

- Checklists, top tips, guidance, caution and comparisons are all useful pieces of information that can also allow you to give value to get value and display your expertise in a practical, customer facing way. Building useful collateral that genuinely adds value and publishing it on your website is more effective than hours of Search Engine Optimisation as it will give you material to send to contacts (and perhaps disseminate more widely).
- It is not impossible, having met someone who mentions a business issue that they are grappling with, to write an article with some useful content and your "take" on the issue together with some practical measures that can address it. You can then upload it to his your website and send it to the person you have just met. Experience shows that they never fail to be impressed with how prescient the article is: "as if it were made for me".

Making Time To Tend Your Network

Previous chapters have set out in some detail the levels of competence required to create and develop a thriving business network. The continuation of this process, once you have established some momentum, should take less effort as you become more adept and as more people champion or broker new introductions for you.

Tending and nurturing your network is therefore a maintenance activity. You may consider how you will plan your time in order to do that effectively. It may be more effective to have short bursts of activity for ten to fifteen minutes daily rather than hope you will clear your schedule for hours at a stretch in order to talk to contacts. It can also be a challenge to stay fresh and spontaneous if give yourself a whole afternoon's worth of phone calls and e-mails in pursuit of your "network".

You will be able to evaluate your progress clearly and easily if you took the time at the outset to get clear about the types of people you wanted to meet and why. In Chapter 6, we emphasised the importance of consciously creating your Lean Marketing Pipeline and having a range of tactics to move your contacts along the pipeline when the time was right. So some of the maintenance of your network will involve keeping your documentation and your pipeline up to date. Once you are regularly making and developing new contacts it is tempting to let your record keeping slip. Your database or CRM programme is only as useful as the information on it: if most of the up to date information is languishing in a desk drawer or (worse still) in your head or in a pile on a shelf at home, all the systems and software in the world cannot help you.

So prioritise your record keeping and formal reviews: they will reassure that you are still on track.

In addition to those more formal reviews of your Pipeline, you can also use small or unexpected pockets of time to make a connection or keep in touch. Unexpectedly delayed or waiting somewhere? You can:

- Scroll through the contacts on your phone to see if it prompts a reason to get in touch. Was X going to the conference next month? Has Y seen the review of that author's new book? Note any action or better still, make a call there and then.
- Check your diary for any upcoming events to which you can invite contacts or arrange to meet people there.
- Tear a relevant or timely article out of a journal or newspaper to send, with a brief hand-written note or post-it, to a contact (See "Saw this and thought of you").
- Subscribe to Amazon Prime and send a useful book or publication to a contact. Use the app on a smartphone and

a book can land on the desk of a recent contact as early as the following working day. If well chosen and appropriate, an inexpensive paperback can deliver an enormous impact.

In this way train and plane delays, waiting for a late arrival or a meeting cancelled at short notice all become opportunities to grow your network, just as some gardeners have a cordless phone and do the odd spot of weeding while on the telephone.

Building A Diverse Network

As with any system, diversity leads to strength and resilience. Think of a mature rainforest: it has strong established trees and all forms of flora and fauna. If you think of your network as an ecosystem, what is its level of diversity? Do you know a lot of the same type of people in a certain job or sector? You may primarily need, for example, to operate in the Built Environment sector or in Education, but how many accountants, bankers or actuaries do you know? Would it be interesting or mutually beneficial for you to get to know some? How might you meet them, where will they be?

Having established your "core" audience with a strong range and depth of knowledge in your own sector, it may be useful and interesting to meet other business people in your community. Working as consultants in the creative and corporate sectors respectively it is notable how similar are many of the challenges and problems faced by clients. Seeking responses to problems and challenges from outside your sector or area of expertise may give you a new approach or an effective solution.

There may be some people, from a business networking perspective, who move out of your ecosystem. This is sometimes because they move away or move jobs (although this is where the virtual networker can continue to nurture contacts even if they move overseas). They may not be as directly relevant to you and your work. It is worth thinking about the people who you may not necessarily "cultivate" on a regular basis but who you may have periodic, generic contact. Consider these people the equivalent of a Christmas Card list. You may only have contact once a year, but it's always good to stay in touch.

Strategically it may be useful to review your network to find candidates to be placed in a holding pattern. It's another tactic in renewing your ecosystem. If you want new growth, or a better shape, you need to prune occasionally.

Be Easy To Help

All of the roles described above have distinct openings for action but think about how you can make it easy for your contacts to tell other people about you. Explain what you do in a vivid and clear way. Avoid jargon and ideally tag your description with a quick story about the results you produce so that the description is memorable. Some people call it an elevator pitch but really what is required is a short memorable, results-based description of you and your work.

As we mentioned in Chapter 5, this attitude to a contact is useful: "Help me understand the value you can offer to the people I know. Tell me so that I can explain it to them and make introductions if there's an opportunity". You can model this behaviour to others: you can share your work in a way that articulates the value you offer and indicates who you want to meet. This makes you easy to help.
Another way to be easy to help is to know what specifically you are looking for from any giving interaction. This can range from

market intelligence, a lead or introduction, a specific opinion or piece of feedback or a need to find out more about a person, business or opportunity. People are often very generous and geared up to asking, "How can I help you, what are you looking for?" It is much more straightforward if you know the answer to that question and you would be amazed at how often people ask it on first meeting.

Serving Your Network

Which leads to the flip side of that behaviour: how you can help the people that you meet. We have already mentioned in Chapter 6 that you can serve your network regardless of your age, experience or level of expertise. New market entrants may have modern approaches and new ideas. They may have an international perspective or bring insight from another sector. The roles described above indicate the manner in which you might serve your network, but the specific things that you can do include:

- **Writing on your subject:** now that weblogs and email newsletters are so abundant, there are many opportunities to put together an article or opinion and to disseminate it on the web. Beware of the pitfall of arriving suddenly in a social media space, writing just one article and then demanding that everyone should read it and spark a heated debate. Online spaces have an etiquette just as spaces in the real world do: make sure you are aware of that etiquette before launching into print. Again, as you would in offline situations, spend a little time observing the behaviours on line – it's called lurking – so that you can behave in a context-appropriate manner.
- **Speaking on your subject:** whether at a seminar, internal training session or other business event outlined

in Chapter 3, there are abundant opportunities to speak and share your expertise. Disseminating new developments, a recap, a introduction to your subject area is often welcome and for some it is easier than writing an article. If you are going to create a talk ensure that it is meticulously researched, crafted, rehearsed and presented. You can always take an article down from the internet or have someone edit it before publishing. On your feet in front of people, you need to get it right first time! Given that many people loathe the very idea of speaking in public, it remains a wonderful opportunity to impress and serve your network. Public speaking is a competence you can cultivate and gain confidence in the same way that you are growing in competence and confidence in networking.

- **Volunteer or work on a committee:** again, many business networking organisations rely on the extra-curricular contribution of their members. This is a powerful way to forge new relationships in your sector, to be at the heart of their events and to influence their agenda. It can be very time-consuming so ensure that you get the right balance of effort and reward if you decide to pursue such an opportunity. Volunteering can be a thankless task, with lots of criticism when things go wrong but little praise for success! The committee itself can create a support system.
- **Host events yourself:** this does not necessarily have to be a high cost or high tech affair. Coffee bars, pubs with event rooms will often make their space available to you. Meet-ups and informal events are common. Even making a regular date to be in a specific place at a certain time can create a regular forum for people to get together (The second Thursday of the month from 5.30 pm in your local coffee shop).

Pipeline Unblockers - What To Do To Get Back In Flow

Common blocks…

- **"I've left it too long to get back in touch…"**
  Has anyone ever contacted you out of the blue – were you happy or annoyed?

- **"Keep phoning/emailing/ etc but they don't answer"**
  Use different channel – can you change the message? Is there some value you can add?

- **Can't think of a reason to get in touch?**
  What value can you add? Can you just call to say, "Hello, how are you?"

- **"Stuck" in a particular loop – can't move conversation on…**
  Keep goals in mind – address it respectfully… Usually it is because something isn't clear – what can you do to clarify? That itself moves the conversation on… Sometimes the "brave honest" conversation can move things on but you can be light about it. It is a business conversation not a dating agency…

- **Stuck because you said you would do something and you didn't.**
  Fess up: apologise and move on… We are all human – so just get in touch – make it up if you can and otherwise say sorry and shake it off.

Final Thoughts

You have now read about all the stages of the networking process. We have explained how to approach this task with intelligence and rigour. We hope that you have learned the fundamentals of this approach and the principles involved in building a network, identifying target contacts and locations, meeting people, establishing a rapport and developing a relationship.

By consciously mapping where you are in your conversation with people as regards the types of conversations (are they business or social), the venues (are we meeting on neutral territory or on their/ my business premises) and the formality of the dialogue (are we talking about specific and real business opportunities) you can measure progress. This measurement may seem artificial at first but this allows you to appreciate your progress. For reluctant networkers it can at least show a tangible return on your investment of time and effort.

Think of what we have discussed in Chapters 1 – 9 as musical scales. The fundamentals of all music. Even the greatest jazz improvisers had to learn their scales at one point. Once you have mastered them you can go out and make these tools your own. Take what has worked for you and improvise: do what works and jettison what was less successful. Do not abandon useful or successful practices or tools simply because you dislike them or they are out of your comfort zone. Can you work out how to make them easier or more comfortable while maintaining the results they produce?

The next two chapters focus on NetworkAbility inside an organisation. Chapter 12 has some hints and tips to refresh your NetworkAbility if it needs a boost.

Chapter 10

The Well-Networked Firm – A Guide for Managers

Consider this: it is extremely possible that investing in your firm's ability to build and capitalise on relationship networks offers the best ROI currently available to you. A full-on programme will probably involve no capital expenditure and could start to bring in results in a few days, as well as creating long-term sustainable value that you can benefit from for years to come.

And the very fact that lots of people dislike networking creates a further advantage to you. By doing things your competition's staff are reluctant to match, you will stand out (and as the supposed unpleasantness of networking is illusory, you won't have to suffer in the process).

This chapter will explain:

- Why relationships are such a powerful strategic factor for many businesses
- How to extend the methods we have shown you to get teams to network
- What a full-on programme might look like
- How to deal with the organisational pitfalls that get in the way of adopting this
- Tips for encouraging networking among your people

Networking and Strategy

Unless you are the 'only shop in town', your business needs sources of sustainable competitive advantage. That means:

- you need to offer services which your buyers see and value as distinct, and that
- the distinctiveness has to be hard to copy.

This is timeless business truth.

If you run a business that brings professional or expert services to your clients and customers, then actually you have few possibilities for distinct and hard-to-copy assets:

1. Your professional, creative and/or expert people
2. Your high-trust relationships with buyers
3. Perhaps, distinct proprietary methodologies (the source of which will be the interaction of 1 & 2).

Again, these are facts of business life, but our observation is that many people pay lip-service to such ideas, so allow us to take a moment to drive the point home.

Figure 10.1 is taken from the work of Alan Weiss and it's a great tool to get leaders to really focus on where they are going to compete (despite the temptation, you can't compete everywhere because you will never reach a critical mass in any particular dimension).

	Competitive	Distinctive	Breakthrough
Product (Purchased tangible)			
Service (Purchased Intangible)			
Relationship (Non-purchased Intangible)			

Figure 10.1. From Process Consulting, Weiss (2002).

The figure shows three kinds of commercial interaction, at three levels of competitiveness. Let's agree some definitions to make sure the figure is clear.

- A product is something of value that is tangible – a physical object – and is paid for by a customer or client.
- A service is something of value that is intangible but that nonetheless is paid for.
- A relationship, in the business context, is again a source of value, but it is not explicitly paid for.

Each of these three types of commercial transaction can happen alone or in combinations (you may be a loyal customer of Waitrose, from whom you always buy your food, partly because of the quality, but also because of the way the staff treat you).

What about the three levels of competitiveness?

- Just Competitive here means 'good enough to get you a seat at the table'.
- Distinctive means that you have an edge which customers value in preference to your competitors.
- Breakthrough means you are so good in that dimension that you have a completely dominant position.

There's a force of gravity that acts from right to left.A breakthrough product (e.g. Sony Walkman in its time) drifts to being distinctive as competitors appear, then to just competitive as new entrants stand on the innovator's shoulders, and ultimately, of course, to uncompetitive (in the Walkman's case, with the arrival of the iPod).

The ideal profile is going to differ depending on your business. And being clear about it is going to help a lot in allocating resources and effort. So what should your profile be?

Many professionals when first shown this framework claim that their objective is to be breakthrough in all three dimensions:

Fig. 10.2. From Process Consulting, Weiss (2002)

	Competitive	Distinctive	Breakthrough
Product (Purchased tangible)			*
Service (Purchased Intangible)			*
Relationship (Non-purchased Intangible)			*

This is actually impossible, because no firm has limitless resources, and while you are trying to be the best at everything, a competitor can apply all its efforts to being best in just one, which is all they need. In fact, pursuing the 'breakthrough in everything' profile is likely to comprehensively exhaust and then undermine the business.

So what profile should you adopt? It's much easier to move from left to right in relationships than it is in products (Or in services for that matter. Many businesses faced with strong competition for their products attempt to compensate through higher levels of service. But service improvements are easy to claim, and are usually straightforward for determined competitors to match).

Fig. 10.3. From Process Consulting, Weiss (2002)

	Competitive	Distinctive	Breakthrough
Product (Purchased tangible)	*		
Service (Purchased Intangible)		*	
Relationship (Non-purchased Intangible)			*

Not only is it easier to create distinctive relationships, it also more beneficial. Think about the great value of unique relationships between buyers and trusted providers of goods and services:

Trust is higher, so

- There's less argument about prices
- It's easier to get paid more quickly
- It's easier sell them other things
- It's easier to use junior staff – the client knows you'll keep an eye on things

Because the relationship is between two individuals

- It's hard to copy – you achieve automatic uniqueness
- You get early warning on upcoming work opportunities
- There's a strong barrier to competition.

Case Study: How A Legal Team Increased Revenue By 10% For Free

One legal team was operating within an extremely competitive part of the banking sector. They were under pressure to grow, and wanted to increase the share of business they received from a major financial institution.

As was traditional, the two partners brought in all the business, and handled all client contact. This created two big problems: first, the partners were flat out and couldn't increase the amount of their time they spent selling. Second, it meant that no one else in team was learning to build the business. If the partners moved or retired, the remaining team would lack the contacts and skills to remain competitive.

Here's how the situation was quickly and cheaply turned around:

- A crash course in simple relationship building skills (the principles explained in this book)
- Mapping the current relationships among the firms' and the clients' people at all levels, as well as the issues and concerns of the various decision-makers. See an example at Figure 11.2 – a Rich Picture.
- Rating the current stage of development of those relationships using a pipeline model, and displaying the combined relationship in such a way as to show current strengths, gaps and opportunities.
- Developing actions with the best chance of strengthening those relationships.
- Implementing actions and then updating the displays.

Actions included partners bringing junior colleagues to meetings and introducing them as 'up-and-coming', mid-level associates seeking out their counterparts in the client organization, and even PAs arranging to meet the client's PAs for lunch.

The results were fast. Over a six month period, a team with seemingly no way to increase its fees without extra hires was able to generate an additional 10% in fees with minimal effort. The results were produced by people who weren't even seriously expected to sell anything, and at no additional cost to their current marketing budget.

Other benefits followed. Partners found that their time was freed up to attend to the relationships with the most critical senior decision-makers. The exercise enhanced the client's perception of the Firm's depth and breadth of service, and strengthened prospects of continuing longer-term business.The project was rolled out within the law firm nationally, with similar results multiplied.

There were also developmental benefits. Individuals and the team reported an increased sense of control of business development and of their relationship to the client in a competitive environment. And with everyone having a real role to play, team building has been accomplished in the best possible way – through shared success in a real-world situation.

People often say things such as 'everyone's a sales person' or 'everyone is in the quality department'. That's great. This technique will give you a way to turn this fine sentiment into action.

We have found that:

- People who are not in traditional sales roles can absolutely win work – clients do not always need to deal with senior executives or official salespeople before they are prepared to give work.
- 'Ones and twos' add up– it's not just about hitting sixes.

Small initial jobs won by junior staff can lead to much large pieces of referral work.

- Teams that coordinate their efforts can quickly win more work from large clients.

Implementing A Business-Wide Approach To External Networking

Telling people to start networking, even when supported by good quality sales training and the right carrots and sticks, will be less successful than hoped for, unless cultural resistance is addressed. Building strong networking skills, and the culture to support their application, is an easy enough course to prescribe, but implementation can mean dealing with considerable resistances. No initiative ever fails at the planning stage. It is always implementation that matters, and many consultants have observed that even an average strategy, well executed, will beat an excellent plan executed without discipline and follow-through.

1. **Establish visible leadership that convinces people 'this is real'** The first step is to establish the key role of leadership. There are only a few people in any organisation who have the credibility to convince others that an initiative is 'real'. Those people are very rarely, if ever, consultants, trainers or HR staff.This means that if you try to delegate the leadership of change to your business-support functions, people just won't join in (or will only be there in body, not spirit). Hiring a sales-training firm, even if it has an excellent reputation, will not do it on its own.

2. **Make sure established partners are on board or are at least prepared not to stand in the way**
   In trying to steer a particular course, there are various tides and currents that can help or hinder progress. These are the cultural factors, prevalent opinions, local received wisdom etc, and they are influenced by many people outside of the formal organisational chart.

It's easy for established partners to undermine plans and not necessarily through concerted or even deliberate effort. Sometimes key influencers 'don't know their own strength'. A raised eyebrow or offhand comment, in response to talk of a new initiative can be enough to discourage juniors from buying in.

A further difficulty arises when juniors get mixed messages about learning and development activities. If they are put on courses by one part of the firm and then, depending perhaps on the topic, pulled off them by someone else at the last minute, so that they never get the training, they develop an acute sense of priorities. Those priorities may or may not match the strategic direction the firm wants to take.

Much of a firm's culture is propagated tacitly. Irrespective of what they are told to do, people copy the conspicuous behaviour of those considered successful. Some of the behaviours inconsistent with a sales culture, including:

- Ditching rehearsals for pitches at the last minute, and then muddling through on the day;
- Turning up for seminars, but chatting to colleagues or established clients rather than engaging with new contacts;
- Relying on a few star 'rain makers', which cultivates a kind of helplessness, underpinned by the idea that only a few people can bring in work.

The implication of these observations is that a lot of consensus-building may be required among the partners before trying to influence the associates and juniors.

Ideally, of course, the partners will be enthusiastically sponsoring the change, but to those less keen, you might say: "With your reputation and contacts, I know you don't need to get into sales, but things are different for the youngsters, and we don't do them any favours if we let them believe that what worked in the good old days will work for them."

3. **Develop and communicate a new view of networking**
   Changing views is an educational rather than training process. Many people have acquired the restrictive view that selling is somehow an unprofessional, somewhat unethical activity that takes advantage of a potential client. In fact, really good high-value salespeople add value beyond that of the goods or service, because they have to understand their clients so well (this is where strong/deep relationships become so important).

   It's interesting to think and act with the idea that the purpose of a professional is to create a client (after all, no clients, no profession). To sell a high-value service effectively, you have to take time to understand, develop and articulate a value proposition to a potential client. The process of doing this is consultative and, by requiring the client to think through and verbalise their issues, brings additional clarity, so adding value over and above the service itself.

   Top sales people are extremely client-focused. As a matter of necessity, they are intimately involved in understanding their client's industry, its underlying economics, current issues and breaking news.

Fig. 10.4 Client Experience

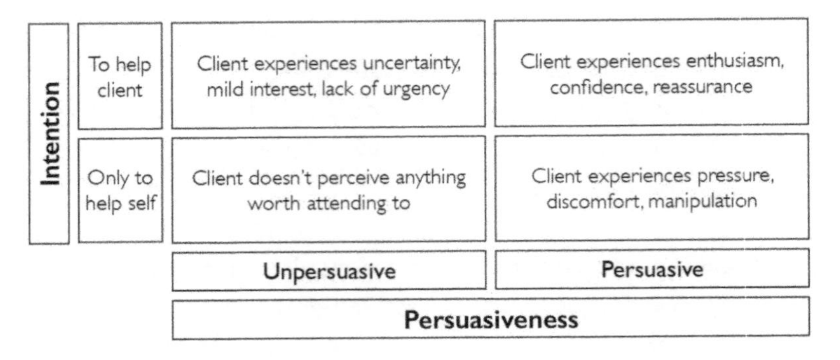

Intention
To help client
Client experiences uncertainty, mild interest, lack of urgency
Client experiences enthusiasm, confidence, reassurance
Only to help self
Client doesn't perceive anything worth attending to
Client experiences pressure, discomfort, manipulation
Unpersuasive
Persuasive
Persuasiveness

Figure 10.4 examines the client's experience of being sold to under various conditions. We use it to reassure people that as long as the salesperson is both persuasive and has a high concern for the client's interests, the usual worries about sales are avoided, the client's experience is positive and the firm's interests are optimally promoted. There are several strategies for getting the new message across:

- High visibility, in-person appearances by leaders and opinion formers are most powerful. These can be formal events and, probably more powerfully, informal – for example, stopping by for a chat about the new initiative. Distributing videos can also help but, in general, beware of overload in remote methods of communication – the photo and scanned signature of the managing partner on every new mail-out is an overused device, for example;
- Gather and tell true stories that make the various values of a sales culture clear and concrete. The values might include being proactive, really listening to clients, having patience and tenacity in cultivating contacts over a long lead time etc. We recently attended a talk by Howard Krais of Eversheds, at which he discussed the power of such stories as part of a

'Visions and Values' initiative at the firm. They work particularly well when told by prominent influencers in person, and you can also record and disseminate them on video and audio;

- Invite clients to visit to talk about sales with your people. Many of them are involved in B2B sales in their own businesses. Their feelings about the role of sales, the process of networking, and the experience of being sold to, are likely to offer credible challenges to old views. Asking clients to perform in this expert capacity can't hurt your relationship with them either;
- At every opportunity, attack the unrealistic idea that 'the quality of work should speak for itself '. Maybe it should, but this idea, which seems to us quite prevalent especially among former A-grade students, is just not how the world works, and is inconsistent with business success.

4. Identify individuals and teams to use as exemplars.

Earlier, we discussed the ways in which people take their lead from the behaviour of key influencers. The use of exemplars turns this dynamic into a powerful way of positively influencing the culture.

Essentially, the idea is to identify up-and-coming, ambitious associates. Coach them to perform in the required way and make sure that they are seen to benefit from doing so. The experience gathered at this stage is also invaluable in piloting the presentation of training programmes for subsequent roll-out.

5. Plan a learning and skill-building programme and evaluate it properly

We once met a senior civil servant who complained of his boss's management style, which included thinking of a memo as a proxy for action. If memos influenced behaviour reliably, management would be easy indeed.

Just as directives are limited in their effect, so, very often, is stand-alone training, especially when trainers parachute in, do their performance, get their happy-sheet scores (which are notorious for having no correlation with business results) and then leave. Yet this way of using training is the norm rather than the exception.

As universal as happy sheets are, does it really matter that much what trainees thought of the training? It follows from our discussion so far that a young professional who doesn't think that they need to sell is probably wrong, and almost certainly has no basis to assess a sales trainer. Sometimes we dislike and resist what we most need to learn. And a good score might just mean that the trainer's personality was agreeable, or that they could tell a good story.

Neither should we get too excited that trainees could demonstrate the skills in the training room. What counts is whether they do new things in the work environment, and those new things lead to improved results.

Minimally, a networking-training programme for professionals should cover:

1. Educating people that relationships are assets (adult learning requires that people know and accept the rationale before they will give something their attention). Emphasise how their self-interest is best served:
2. How to track towards business;
3. Interpersonal influencing skills.

Beware Of Allowing 'Soft Marketing'

As necessary as building relationships is, it can easily end up as what venture capitalist John Handley, calls 'soft marketing'. Soft marketing is Handley's way of describing pleasant social interaction, which, although done in the name of business development, doesn't end up yielding work.

It's a well-known problem for sales people in all sectors. It's very common for sales meetings to be pleasant social affairs that lead only to an agreement to 'keep in touch'. Experienced sales professionals are focused on finding some way to move forward, perhaps not all the way to a sale in one go (high-value networking often involves multiple meetings), but some definite step nearer.

The key value of the pipeline is its function as a focus for attention; networking and business development is a longish game, and the pipeline framework directs the attention of everyone to the ongoing activity of turning contacts into clients using a logical, sequential and manageable set of steps.

From a managerial perspective, it is important to have such a framework because it gives you a way of tracking, discussing and coaching individual (and group) performance. It also gives you the opportunity to reinforce and reward behaviours, which, although they have yet to yield a huge deal, are moving in the right direction and are evidence of people building their skills.

As a further development, we have recently been experimenting with ways of valuing likely future earnings from a given pipeline (in much the same way as drug companies are valued, based on their development pipelines). This gives quantitative data that focuses the mind on building the asset value of business relationships.

Interpersonal Influencing Skills

To advance through the sales pipeline requires person-to-person influencing skills, and perhaps this is the area where old cultural stereotypes about slick-talking and patter can most easily assert themselves.

Actually effective sales couldn't be further away from the slick-patter approach – rather than talking too much, effective sales people ask a lot of questions and listen carefully to the answers. Various questioning models exist, but the successful ones share an emphasis on teasing out the undesirable consequences of inaction. Rightly or wrongly, many decisions on a proposal are based not on what the benefits would be if you went ahead, so much as the pain you would experience if you did nothing.

Of course, asking about problems can upset, rather than motivate, the other party. Any good networking programme should foster the interpersonal skills needed to ask about the dangers of inaction, without upsetting the seller.

Role Conflict And Switching

A number of lawyers have told us that they find it hard to switch roles from being a professional adviser to being a salesperson. The skills required of each role are different. Typically in the adviser role, one takes the stance of expert, and the style of communication is one of targeted questions (often to quickly exclude irrelevant information), and of telling the client the answer.

In a successful networking process, the balance of expert power is more equal, and the seller often has to ask questions from the stance of 'not knowing'. The style is very different and can conflict with the legal-adviser stance. This incompatibility can be a source of discomfort. People benefit from reassurance that, when networking, there is no loss of respect or authority in asking questions in a more open-ended style – it is alright not to know the answer in advance.

One litigator we know told us that he is aware that he shifts roles and style when involved in a mediation, and that he needed a way to make a similar switch to the role of salesperson or networker. A good training programme should help people make such shifts.

6. Put in place the right cultural reinforcers

Better behaviours will happen not only when people have the right skills but also, crucially, when it's in their perceived best self interests to do them.

There are a number of factors to consider, including at least:

1. Links to promotion criteria;
2. Managing the conflict between fee-earning time and business-development time.

Common Cultural Blockers

The presence of any of the following can undermine your efforts to create a networking culture:

- Certain types of established partners don't personally need to change, even though their firm does, because they have a strong repeat client base;
- Associates have not woken up to the commercial reality that it is no longer good enough to be a good technical lawyer;
- 'Brain surgeon' types who simply lack the personal wherewithal to develop the requisite skills in a realistic timeframe. (It may be better to give these people 'resident

expert in this field' status, and sell their expertise as a firm resource, rather than expect them to sell themselves. This option should only be reserved for those with extreme technical competence.)

Your Initial Plan Of Attack

- Make it plain that networking services is how the firm makes money;
- Hire enterprising, ambitious people who are interested in building a business that they will one day be able to share in;
- Train them and coach them (or have them trained and coached) in the most persuasive and sophisticated possible sales techniques;
- Use the best possible sales-management techniques – there's a huge amount of pragmatic, effective knowledge that's been gained on this in other sectors. Overall, the point at which you acquire staff is the easiest time to make clear that the job does not just involve receiving instructions and dispatching excellent advice. It also includes key business functions: attracting and creating relationships with clients; giving exemplary service; negotiating fees; and knowing that the sale's not made until the bill's been paid.

Case Study: Culture And Incentives

A common pitfall in new growth initiatives is to expect people to pursue them while making no concession to their existing short-term delivery commitments.

For example, a group of associates in a property consultancy were participating in a project to boost business development. The partners were delighted with the rapid initial impact on the local marketplace. However, those associates who enthusiastically embraced the new initiative and began actively marketing and networking soon realised that they were doing so to the detriment of their personal utilization performance relative to their colleagues who stayed in the office clocking up billable hours.

They quickly stopped networking again, and found all sorts of creative excuses to stay in the office, until the partners finally agreed to a relaxation in utilization targets in return for their renewed participation in the project.

Ten Things You Can Do To Support Your People In Their Networking

We've found that the following easy-to-implement (and cost-free) suggestions can really help your people to quickly become more confident and effective networkers.

1. **Reinforce the *behaviours* that are moving in the right direction, rather than waiting for the results.** Networking is a medium-to-long-term investment. Actions

have to be taken consistently for a long time before tangible (£££) results appear. Few, especially early in their careers, can keep going without some external reinforcement and encouragement that it's going to work.

2. **Catch people doing things right**. This is the secret to reinforcement. If you see someone go up to a lonely guest at one of your seminars or events and 'rescue' them, make sure to reinforce it immediately.

3. **Reinforce quickly.** People are surprisingly responsive to simple and immediate recognition of what has been done – a nod, a "Well done". A good appraisal six months later won't do the same trick.

4. ***Take* people networking rather than sending them.** This will help the shyer people, enable them to see what happens, and enable you to give them a kick-start through judicious introductions.

5. **Give the seal of approval**. Introduce people with more than just a name. e.g.
   To client: "This is James B. He's been doing great work with me for two years now." To James: "This is Jane D from XYZ Plc – she's a good person to know."

6. **Make the rules of engagement clear.** Make sure your people are clear about who they can and cannot talk to. If they are unsure, most young professionals won't take a chance on upsetting a senior – but if they become conditioned to timidity, they will never be much good at business development.

7. **Once you are confident in people, give them space to talk**. Having introduced an employee to someone, if appropriate, take a step back so that they can make an initial impression.

8. **Encourage people to cultivate existing contacts**. It's more comfortable for shy people, and generally more profitable, to cultivate a few high quality relationships than to be a 'face on the scene'. Coach them on their progress in filling up and moving people through a pipeline: "How are you doing with that contact at XYZ?"

9. **Encourage people to seek out up-and-coming talent of their level at the client's organisation.** Consider asking your client to suggest people. Explain that it's in the client's interest to facilitate better two-way communication.

10. **Offer war stories of how you have developed client relationships.** Let people know how you won your clients and how the relationship has developed. Give them a sense of the timescale and commitment involved.

Chapter 11

Networking for Improved Organizational Performance

In Chapter 10, we described the following benefits for internal performance.

- Improved leadership
- Improving customer experience.
- Accelerating cross-functional working.
- Reducing them-and-us conflict.
- Increasing innovation.

Networking And Market Intelligence

Wise leaders cultivate multiple sources of information – they certainly don't rely entirely on formal reports to tell them what is going on. The newspapers are full of examples of the organizational underperformance, even failure, which follows when managers allow themselves to be cut off from reality.

Conversely, some of the most dramatic improvements we have ever seen in either business or individual performance were achieved by changing who leaders were talking and listening to. The intervention might have been described up in various ways but it you stripped away the protocols and management jargon and just filmed the client 'before and after', you'd see that the difference that made the difference was new conversations with better-informed people – i.e. effective internal and external networking.

Senior executives run the risk of living in a world mediated by memos. If you are not extremely careful, you can end up talking only to your direct reports, the board, investors and advisors. The consequence is insulation from reality.

One MD was shocked to read in a trade magazine that his number one competitor had been awarded a contract he hadn't even known was available to bid on. This was a substantial company – with an excellent reputation for its engineering – in a B2B market where just ten to twenty contracts were available per year.

Another CEO had been begging his engineers to build a slimmer version of a ventilation unit used in commercial buildings, only to be assured that the physics meant it was impossible. Imagine his surprise when he finally left his office and went to a trade show, to find the competition displaying a 'physically impossible' slim ventilator. He kicked his display stand over in anger in full view of the trade show delegates. You can imagine his horror and embarrassment. The competitor was out with the product now. How long would it take to work out what they were doing and get something into production? And, even more worrying, just how far behind the competition were they?

So often I find – and, ominously, colleagues in the turnaround profession say the same – that answers to serious challenges to a business are likely to be found in the heads of frontline staff, customers or even people like trade journalists – but they have never been asked.

There is no need to seek deep psychological explanations for all this. We can observe the human tendency to cut ourselves off from reality, even when the stakes are as high as they could be. The French High Command at the start of WW2 – at the Château de Vincennes – was described by one staff officer as 'a submarine without a periscope' and we know how that went.

As it is for Generals, so for businesses, individual executives and professionals. The business people who I've observed progressing, or even in these volatile times just surviving, are those who seek out informed conversation outside the self-sealing information bubble that constantly tries to envelop them.

Improved Engagement

Who Should You Network With In Order To Increase Engagement?

Amazing but true: people buy companies and don't meet the people for weeks or months. This is the most effective way to fuel a rumour mill. And while people are focused on the rumours, they are not focusing on customers. The meeting process doesn't have to be in the form of official presentations (in fact these are unlikely to be believed most of the time).

Some ideas:

- Avoid coming over like a visiting dignitary
- Leave the PowerPoint behind
- Have lunch in the staff cafeteria.

Remember that actions speak louder than words. In particular, you must meet the key influencers early. In any organisation there will be certain opinion leaders who others look to for guidance. But these are often not the "official" bosses.

Remember the two marines charged with murder in the film *A Few Good Men*? One is the charismatic and purposeful Lance Corporal Dawson, and the other is Private First Class Downey, who is naïve and has some learning difficulties. He is described as "idolising" the Lance Corporal. Whenever something in the court proceedings occurs that he doesn't understand, or that frightens him, the

Private turns to Dawson (not the judge or even his own defence team although they are all officers) as the source he trusts in order to find out what is going on and what to do about it.

The way to change organisational culture is to find and influence the influencers. To influence Private Downey, you have to win over Lance Corporal Dawson. Similarly, if a respected supervisor thinks you are ok, you will get the support of everyone who looks up to him or her.

So how do you figure out who to focus on?

Questions To Ask Yourself About Stakeholders

- Who is actually in the organization?
- Who does the work?
- Who sets goals?
- Who do people look to to decide what is 'real'?
- Who does the organization interact with outside its boundary (customers, suppliers, influencers)
- What's on their minds?
- Who do they get on with?
- Who do they experience friction with?

Represent The Information Visually With A Rich Picture

Some conventions to note: individual and groups are represented as stick people. Their concerns, objectives etc are captured in thought-bubbles. Lines of alliance or conflict are labelled with smiles or crossed swords as appropriate. Influential observers (media, regulatory authorities etc) are shown by eyeballs. Beyond these basics, you are free to make up further icons as you go.

Fig 11.1

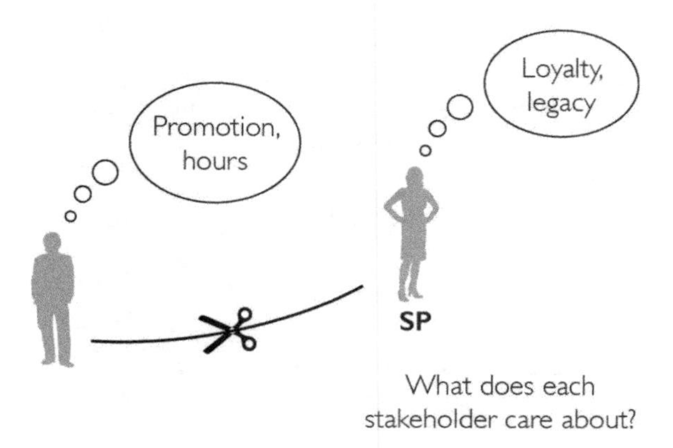

As simple as this seems, the effect of a Rich Picture can be dramatic. On a number of occasions we have done little more than re-presented a situation to a group of directors using this format for them simply to say: "Oh, ok, the solution is now obvious." And even when that doesn't happen, the resulting discussion and investigation is always more penetrating and insightful than if we had relied on dense sequential narrative information.

Beyond the outline above, there are very few rules for drawing Rich Pictures, although I notice that some people are much better at producing useful ones than others (you improve with practice).

Fig 11.2. A Rich Picture

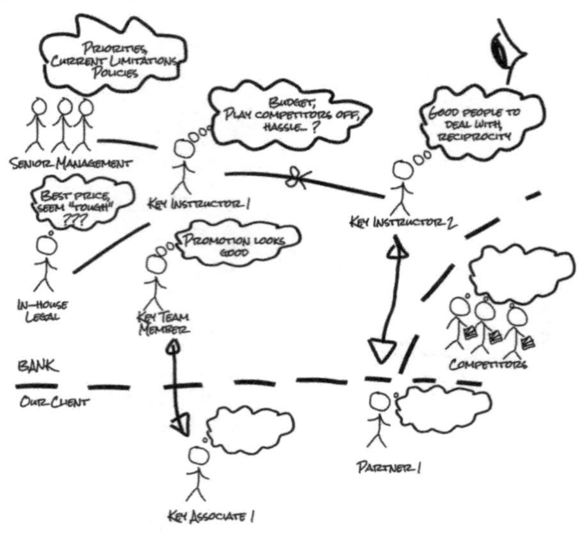

Make An Influence Plan

In Chapter 8 we evaluated prospective client contacts in order to decide how much time to allot them. The same principle applies here, but the filter is different.

Fig 11.3. Power/interest matric

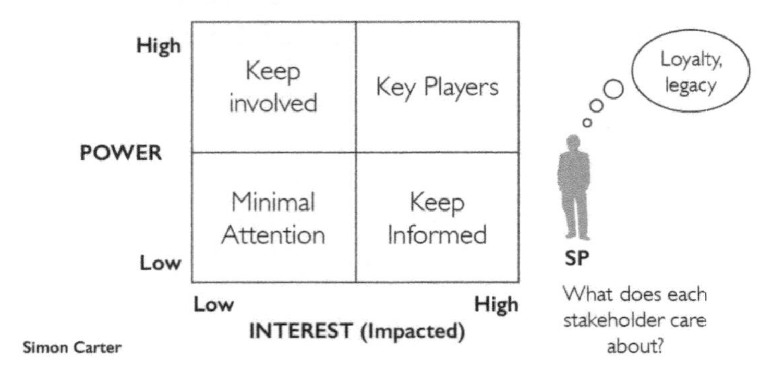

Accelerating Cross-Functional Working

In his book *The Performance Papers: Incisive Briefings for Busy Leaders*, Andy discusses the issue of accelerating implementation by influencing across departments, noting that one of the most frustrating and wasteful drags on implementation speed arises when teams having to wait for people in other internal departments to do things. The full chapter is available for free at www.bassclusker.com, along with details about the book.

Andy lists the following ten tactics for expediting projects, negotiating silos and generally managing "stakeholders". Some focus on tasks and some on relationships. You don't need to do them all. In fact it's best to pick the one or two which most suit the situation and the people you are dealing with.

Make sure your project teams are familiar with these principles – you will see how all of them depend on, or are enhanced by, strong internal networks.

1. **Sell it from their point of view** How will helping you help them? Will it make their scheduling easier, make them look good, or even just get you off their back?

2. **Identify the natural conditions under which they would willingly help you, and act to establish them** Ask yourself: "Under what circumstances would the other person do what I want naturally and quickly?" For example, if your accounts payable policy is to accept any early payment discounts offered, and your order is being sat on by the relevant functionary, say, "I need your help to take this discount for early payment before it expires."

3. **Identify in advance what and who could stall your project, and put plan-protecting actions (both "preventive" and "contingent/insurance") into place** For example, if you know from past experience that a particular manager has a talent for raising annoying queries which hold projects up (perhaps as a way of feeling important) you are going to need to use some guile. Speak to them way before they are scheduled to be involved in the project to get their input – ask them to tell you all the potential problems with your plans and ask for recommendations (preventive action). Then ask them if you may call on them to help troubleshoot any unforeseen issues that inevitably will arise in a project of this nature (insurance action).

4. **Clarify responsibilities and nail down potential ambiguities** When you said you needed it by Friday, what precisely are you asking them to agree to? Are you thinking lunchtime, while they are thinking 5.15pm?

5. **Create obligations by confirming the resources you are mobilising** Eg send an email saying, "Thanks for agreeing to X. I'm visiting the client on Friday and will incorporate your comments while I am on the train so please can you confirm you will get them to me by noon."

6. **Make it easy for them to do what you want** One of the secrets of success in direct marketing, and websites such as Amazon, is to make it really easy for people to respond. You can use the same ideas to expedite your project – it's a little more work for you, but if they are very busy or very senior, it can make the difference, so it could still be worth it. Simple example: if you are chasing someone who is supposed to phone you to discuss a document, include the document

again when you chase them, and send your phone number again too. Just forward the original email and include your signature file. If you don't do this, the other person has to look back though their inbox to find the document, dig your phone number out etc. They are more likely to put it on a to-do list where it will languish for days.

7. **Influence the influencers** Even if you are very senior, in a large matrix organisation, you may not be able to influence the blocking party directly. But someone can. Figure out early on who has the requisite clout: it may be their boss, it may be a mutual friend, it may be an informal opinion leader in their department who has influence just by virtue of personality, and it will often be a secretary. Build an informal influence network and use it.

8. **Work with gatekeepers and assistants** I am sometimes amazed by the lack of astuteness of people who are rude to, or dismissive of, gatekeepers and assistants. It is unacceptable behaviour in itself, but it is also plain daft. Secretaries can get all sorts of things fast-tracked, or alternatively cause them to languish at the bottom of an in-tray.

9. **Invest in relationships "offline"** It's easy, as we have noted, to fall in to the trap of assuming that the other person is blocking you on purpose. Often they are just snowed under themselves. Taking the time to build a relationship with them helps in two ways: a) you realise that they are unlikely to be blocking you on purpose; b) you have more influence when you need it.

10. **Involve them in your plan protection – once you have a good relationship.** This is the ideal situation. Early in the project you get together and discuss the sorts of issues mentioned above together. Remember to couch it in their best interest: "Look I know your team members are really busy and I'd like to see if we can find ways to smooth out the inevitable demands this project will create. Shall we get together and figure out how to make it go as easily as possible?" Then work out your plan promoting and plan protecting actions together. Arrange a "red telephone" so you can call if there's a problem.

Chapter 12

Fifty Ways To Boost Your Networking Immediately

Finally, here are fifty key strategies for networking effectively:

1. Be a source of value to new and existing contacts. Provide information, articles, briefings, introductions.

2. Finesse the business card swap. A lot of people we work with seem to get hung up about swapping cards. There emphasis is on 'closing' rather than providing value. If early in a conversation with a new contact you explore and listen for the needs they have, and you identify an opportunity to help with that need (thereby giving value), then it's easy to say "I've got something I think you'll find helpful. Give me your card and I'll send it you".

3. Know why you are there – showing up is not enough.

4. Be a broker. Inexperienced networkers often feel under pressure to sell to each person they meet at the first conversation. A much more comfortable (and productive) attitude is to take the role of an introducer or broker. So your attitude (which you don't have to say out loud) is "help me understand what you need, and what you offer, and maybe I can put you together with another of my contacts". If you effect a successful introduction, you are in credit with two parties, and if you become known as a broker, your networking will get easier as people seek you out.

5. Ask good questions. Chapter 6 has more information about this.

6. Visit new groups as a guest. And be selective about which

groups you join. Many are just social clubs who talk about business more than they do it.

7. Join a committee. Joining something like a trade association committee is great strategy for people who find social smalltalk difficult, but are confident when there is a substantive task to do. The meetings provide social structure, you interact with new contacts in the course of the work, people get to find out about what you can do, and you make a contribution at the same time.

8. Volunteer for a non-profit organisation. Volunteering for a non-profit organisation puts you in contact with a wide range of people from a variety of sectors, and can have significant personal and professional development benefits in addition to its value for networking. As Peter Drucker puts it, "You have responsibility, you see results, and you quickly learn what your values are. There is no better way to understand your strengths and discover where you belong than to volunteer in a non-profit".

9. Be the speaker. If you speak at an event, even for free, you will be approached by new people who are already have a shared interest with you.

10. Act like a host. Introduce other people to each other at events and generally try to make their experience easier and more comfortable.

11. Always leave people in a better state than you found them. Use the conversation skills from Chapters 7 and 8.

12. Maximise the value of conferences by thinking ahead. Contact

speakers and fellow delegates from your target list ahead of the conference and see if you can connect with and meet them during the conference.

13. Make sure your LinkedIn profile is up to standard. Get a friend or colleague to draft a biography if you are too modest in a self-penned bio.

14. Share content with a 'Saw this and thought of you' message. This is easier than ever with online tools, but a good old fashioned tear-out from the newspaper is more unusual and will stand out as a result.

15. Be a mentor. The best mentors often get more out the relationship than their mentees.

16. Teach. Whether at adult education, for a college or university,

17. Write a blog. A guest post if you don't want to maintain your own.

18. Talk to PAs. Good PAs are often the best networked people in an organization. They very often know more about what is going on across the organization than their bosses.

19. Talk to interns and placement students. People often talk freely in front of placement students – the way some people do in front of waiters – because they don't think they count. Their rudeness in this regard means that interns are often very well informed about organizational politics, new initiatives and operational problems.

20. Talk to security guards and cleaners.

21. Invest in a few good photographs of you to use in online profiles or on blogs/bylines.

22. Look yourself up on a couple of different search engines to manage your online reputation

23. Talk to people who work in 'difficult' departments. Understand what is going on in back office or support teams.

24. Ask people their opinions on business or current affairs news of the day. Reserve this for people who seem likely to have one though, and don't be obscure in your selection of topic, or you might embarrass them if they don't know what you are talking about.

25. Give value to get value.

26. As you move people through the pipeline, ask for small, easy things to start with.

27. Ask senior or powerful people if you can 'run something by them'. It's easy for them to say yes, and most people like being consulted in this way.

28. Use unexpected pockets of time to contact someone by phone or email.

29. Join Amazon Prime – send a well chosen book to a prospect at a moment's notice.

30. Run your own event or set up a regular time and place to connect with people.

31. Take two contacts who don't know one another to lunch. Pick up the tab.

32. Create some valuable collateral for your website – top tips, checklists or guidance.

33. Chose online locations wisely – senior executives rarely lurk on Facebook.

34. Be easy to help – know what to say when someone asks "How can I help you?" or "What are you looking for".

35. Read a news report immediately before going to an event.

36. Vary the sources of your information from time to time.

37. Arrive at networking events early.

38. Get comfortable with surroundings – it's easier to talk to people when there are fewer in the room.

39. Watch your alcohol intake – beware the automatic top-up.

40. Don't be the last to leave – you look like you haven't got anything else to do.

41. Note what you promised to send someone on the back of their business card.

42. Follow up all commitments promptly – the same day if possible.

43. Get a card scanning app.

44. If you find you are at an event and not in the mood – cut your losses and go and do something more useful.

45. Ask organisers for introductions to people you want to meet.

46. Before a first coffee – Google the company for news or useful intelligence.

47. Also look up the person you are meeting and ask them something about their profile.

48. Don't forget the Three Second Rule – just introduce yourself.

49. Look for people to talk to rather than groups of people you can't join. Approach people standing on their own.

50. Don't bust into a conversation that is clearly in full flow – it creates a bad impression – look for more open groups.

Bringing Networkability To Your Business

This book is based on working with thousands of business professionals and entrepreneurs both nationally and internationally. Its step-by-step approach can be taught and developed in a variety of contexts and across a range of experience and settings. Andy Bass of Bass Clusker and Helga Henry of Birmingham Hippodrome can work with you and your team to bring all the benefits of a highly connected, highly leveraged and focussed network to your business. Contact details are avaliable at www.NetworkAbilitybook.com. Please call or email to discuss what might be possible for your organisation if your staff doubled *their* NetworkAbility in 70 days.

You can access useful articles, checklists and further information including dates where Helga and Andy are speaking on this topic, at www.NetworkAbilitybook.com. It is regularly updated with relevant content to enhance your understanding and inspire you to fulfil all 70 days of this practical programme.

This publication is also available for bulk purchase for your company, division or team. Contact us to place your order or search for us on www.amazon.co.uk.

Appendix I:

Further Information On The Top Beneficiaries Of Networking

Networking For Fee-Earning Professionals

For fee-earners in professional service firms (lawyers, accountants, architects, surveyors, consultants), networking and relationship-building is non-negotiable. A professional (and indeed a professional firm) has only two significant assets:

- the ability to advise on and perform complex technical tasks
- client relationships.

Technical ability is rarely the difference that makes the difference. Few client issues are so complex that only a few 'rocket scientists' can manage them, and anyway, there are loads of clever people in the professions. You need to be technically competent in order to get a seat at the table, but if you want to eat, you need to be, or learn to be, 'commercial', too.

Still unconvinced? Just look at your firm and see who is getting promoted to partner. Unless you are in a very stuffy old firm, it's the people who are bringing in business (and if that's not the case, you should consider moving quickly).

Figure A1.1. represents the usual path of progression in a professional firm:

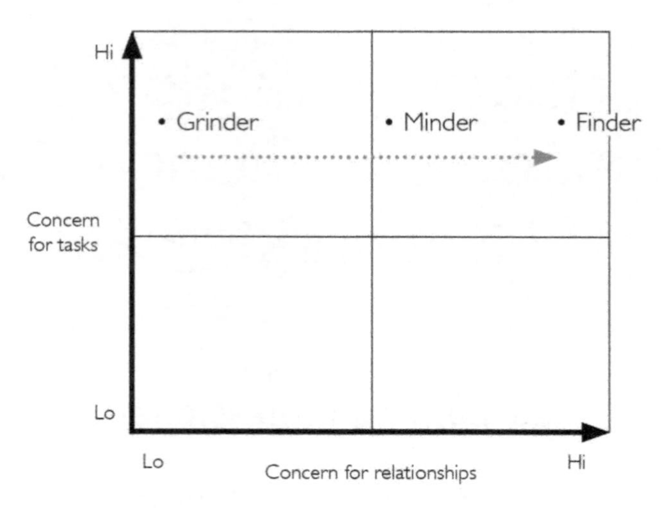

Figure A.1.1 Progression Path © Andy Bass 2005

The figure uses the traditional labels (popularised by David Maister) of "Finders, Minders and Grinders". Finders (partners or people likely to become one) get the work in and advise or at least "lead" on the difficult bits. Minders (often called Associates) manage the work, and Grinders (junior fee earners of one sort or another) do the routine tasks and polish their skills. As you move up, your concern moves from just getting the tasks right, to the relationship aspects: first managing people and then nurturing and developing client contact.

And here too is a hint of the difficulty. Most professionals spend the first twenty to twenty-five years of their lives advancing by being really good at tasks tightly specified by other people: throughout school, GCSEs, A-Levels, University, Professional Qualifications and their initial years Post Qualification. In all of these activities, 100% perfection can be clearly specified, and by many people, quite often met.

But there comes a point where you have to balance your task ability with relationship skills. And relationship building is not a tightly specified task. Perfection is impossible, and seeking perfection is actually dysfunctional because it takes too long!

Precise people in particular really need tools to help nail things down as much as possible. We have worked extensively with young (and not so young) professionals on these challenges, and you will find much from those experiences contained within these pages.

Networking For Small, Expertise-Based Or Creative Firms And Consultancies

Let's not beat around the bush: for these kinds of businesses, you either network or you are dead in the water. Not only will networking be a primary – if not the primary – source of your clients, but also, the unique relationships you and your associates build will be key elements of how you set yourselves apart from the competition. And that competition can be fierce indeed.

And for small expertise-based businesses, networks bring more than sales. They provide vital support structures unavailable outside large corporates:

- Informal access to professional advice
- Mastermind Groups which can act as sounding-boards and sources of coaching
- Mentors

One client, the MD of a media group, attests to just how important effective networking can be.

"Getting the most out of networking is a vital skill for people at any stage in their career, and good networkers can have a hugely positive effect on a business. Working in a busy media agency my team are often out and about meeting new contacts, but converting them to business leads is the real challenge.

Through training, my team were able to develop their approach and, crucially, gain a more insightful understanding of the new business pipeline, how to develop meaningful business relationships and 'getting to yes'. As a result, I now have a more empowered sales force to support in building the company and reaching our aspirations for growth."

Networking For Success In A Corporate Career

Networking is not just vital for business results. Building contacts is essential for any individual who wants to build a corporate career. "Okay," you may be thinking, "they are just saying 'it's not what you know – it's who you know'. But I don't want to get on because people are doing me favours; I want to do it on merit."

This is an admirable motivation, and as we have already intimated, we have definitely seen organizations which are deeply flawed because too many 'players' get promoted, leaving much more competent peers in their wake. Best-kept secrets tend to stay a secret. It's not unheard of for excellent and deserving candidates to be passed up by promotion committees because none of the senior managers around the organization had heard of them. In fact it happens a lot more often than you might think. If you hate 'players', then you must learn how the game is played so you can avoid them rising simply on the basis of the 'pull' they have generated.

So we are not saying 'it's not what you know – it's who you know', we are saying: 'it's what you know, first and foremost, and then it's also who you know – do you know people who can say 'yes', who can open doors, who can vouch for you so you can get a chance to show your skills?'

To some this is obvious. For example, many of the MBA students we have worked with were not aiming to start up their own businesses or bring in work for a professional services firm. They were looking to improve their networking skills in order to seek executive appointments. They recognised the need to build their networking abilities to get on in their careers.

Some people are still tempted to just let the company they work for worry about their progress. This is a dangerously complacent attitude. Think of it this way: when the airline industry first got going, people used to talk about 'The Jet Set' – rich and privileged people who travelled on expensive scheduled flights. In the 1970s, package holidays began to open up the world of travel to people of more modest means. And while there are all kinds of package holidays, many of them tend to treat their punters like items to be processed. That's not everyone's cup of tea – some people like to write their own ticket. The good thing about being an independent traveller is that you don't have to take what you are given.

We're often surprised by the mindset of employees who treat employment like a package holiday and just take what's on offer. Here are some of the reasons why that is a bit daft:

- **There are lots of well-qualified, highly motivated competitors.** UK and US business schools are chock-a-block with hard-working students from emerging market countries. Many educational institutions in those same countries are twinning with elite long-established traditional universities to offer degrees in major East Asian cities. These guys all speak English as well as their mother tongue, and often a couple of other languages too. They are willing to travel, which suits global corporations, and are highly motivated by the new opportunities – maybe more than their peers from old economy countries. And they can do maths.
- **Many jobs, contracts and projects are not advertised, or are secretly shaped around a favourite candidate.** This may sometimes be against company policy, or even illegal, but it's hard to spot or prove. It's often well worth an employer's while, too: hiring decisions are a tremendous risk, so it's natural to want to give jobs to people you know. It's hard to compete against a candidate who is benefiting from this dynamic. If you just apply through the standard HR channels, you will be an application form, not a person.
- **Good businesses and executives will always be interested in acquiring talent, even when they are telling HR there is a hiring freeze.**This is another fact of life that you may not realise. Clever, qualified candidates might not be that rare, but really good, reliable savvy ones are, and switched-on executives will find a way to grab them.
- **Opportunities always exist for people prepared to make things happen, rather than wait and take what's on offer.**

Rather than describing yourself as proactive on your LinkedIn profile, it is more effective to demonstrate it in your behaviour.

- **Better to be the CEO of our own career rather than a 'human resource' (a commodity) to be hired or fired.** Sadly, the language of management does tend to commoditise people, often referring to them as headcount, talent, FTEs (full time equivalents) or 'cost' (as in, "We have concluded after a strategic review that we need to take 35% of cost out of the business."). If you want to be treated as a self-determined human being in the often-impersonal world of business, it will be up to you to make the human connections.

Most if not all of these dynamics will affect your career at one time or another. In order to deal with them, a strong network makes it much easier.

Case Study

Jane (not her real name) was a team manager in the shared services centre of a large corporation. She was managing a team of around thirty people doing important but quite routine transaction processing. She was good at it, was trusted by her boss as a dependable operator, and was well liked by both her staff and her clients. But it was this aspect of her personality – that she thrived on client contact more than the transaction processing – that was making her feel unfulfilled in her current role. She decided that she would like to move into an account management role in another division of the business, something she and her peers agreed she would be well suited for. At her recent appraisals, she had raised this with her boss, and they had agreed it as a medium term aim on her development plan. However, she was starting to think that her manager was humouring her (in fact she began to worry that he was paying lip-service to her ambitions because he didn't want to lose her from her current role: this happens a lot).

A chance conversation with a colleague led to a meeting with a female director from another line in the business. The director recognised the potential blockage to Jane's progress and offered her some mentoring advice and assistance:

- a suggestion to join the company's women's network and see if she could strike up a relationship with some account handlers,
- an introduction to a sympathetic learning and development specialist who could advise on the company's policy about lateral moves and could offer training,
- a recommendation to get a mentor who could help her navigate the ins and outs, and if necessary help her with her

own boss – including suggestions about negotiating with him about how she would groom her own successor to be ready to take over when she moved on.

It took about eighteen months for Jane to then make the transition, and to do so in a way which enabled the business to assimilate the change.